Meatballs and Dead Birds

Meatballs and Dead Birds

**A PHOTO GALLERY OF
DESTROYED JAPANESE AIRCRAFT
IN WORLD WAR II**

James P. Gallagher

STACKPOLE
BOOKS

Copyright © 2004 by Michael C. Muller

Published by
STACKPOLE BOOKS
5067 Ritter Road
Mechanicsburg, PA 17055
www.stackpolebooks.com

All rights reserved, including the right to reproduce this book or portions thereof in any form or by any means, electronic or mechanical, including photocopying, recording, or by any information storage and retrieval system, without permission in writing from the publisher. All inquiries should be addressed to Stackpole Books, 5067 Ritter Road, Mechanicsburg, Pennsylvania 17055.

Printed in the United States of America

10 9 8 7 6 5 4 3 2 1

FIRST EDITION

Library of Congress Cataloging-in-Publication Data

Gallagher, James P.
  Meatballs and deadbirds : a photo gallery of destroyed Japanese aircraft in World War II / James P. Gallagher.— 1st ed.
    p. cm.
  ISBN 0-8117-3161-8
  1. Airplanes, Military—Japan—Pictorial works. I. Title.
TL685.3.G245 2004
940.54'4952—dc22
                    2004016061

To the U.S. Army Air Force's ground crews in the Pacific War, who, under the damnedest conditions imaginable, managed to keep our war birds flying against a determined enemy.

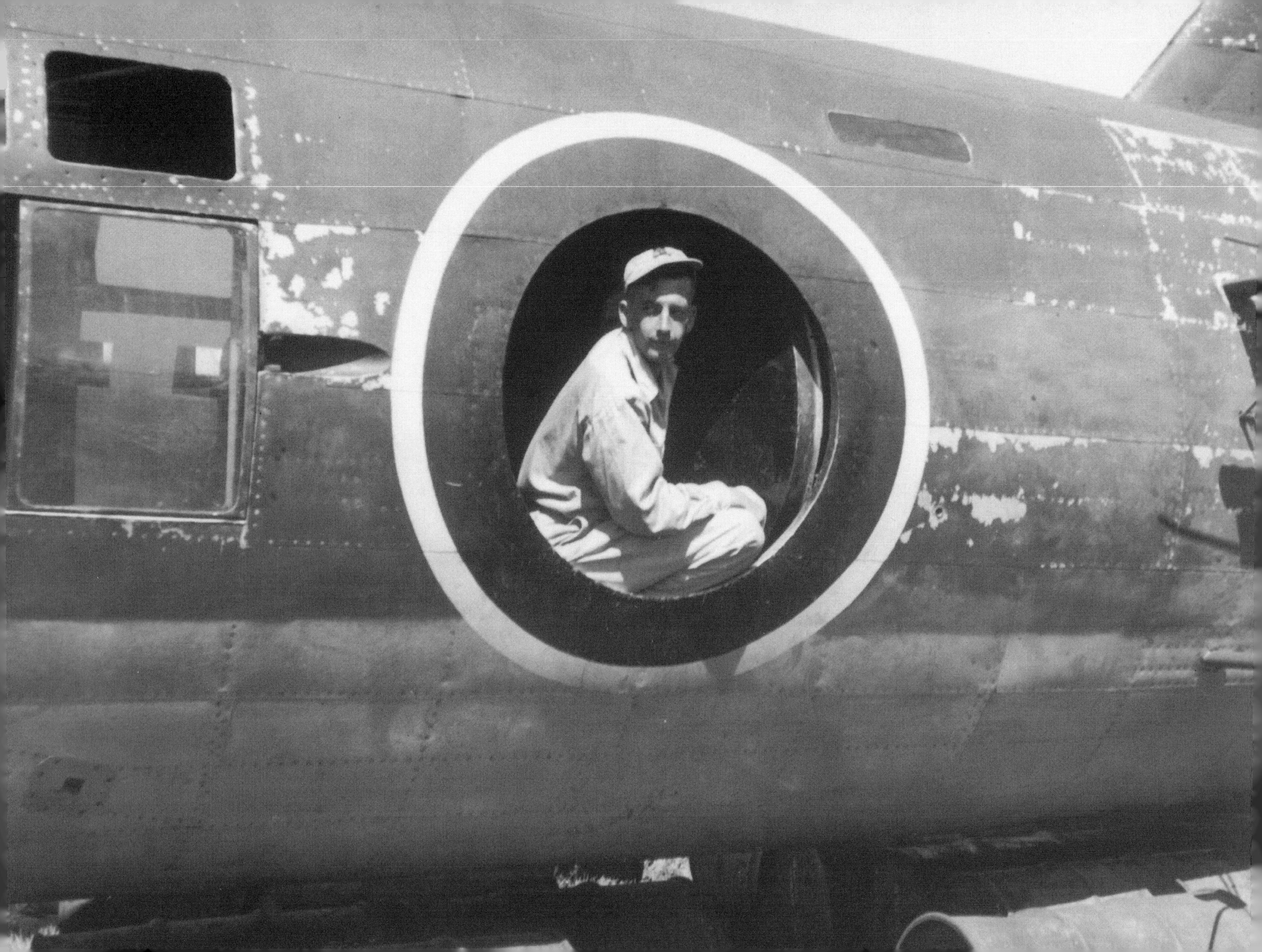

CONTENTS

Foreword by Randy Lutz ix
Introduction xi

A Glance at the Pacific War 1
The "Zero" 7
"Betty" the Bomber 13
B-29 Decoy 19
The Aichi D3A "Val" 21
The "Nell" 23
An Unforgettable Japanese Warbird 25
The "Dinah" 27
Dead "Lilys" of the Airfields 29
"Clipped Wings": "Ann" and "Sonia" 31
The "Tony" 33
A Touch of Americana in the Japanese Air Forces 37
Warbirds—Old and Retired 41
Warbirds—Lost and Found 43
Airfield Construction 47
And "Kate" Begot "Jill" 49

The "Radial Tony": A Plane with No Name? 53
Fighter Protection 55
The Incredible "Weapon": The Suicide Attack ... 59
Was There a "Favorite" Suicide Airplane in the
    Japanese Air Forces? 65
Variations on a Plane by Nakajima: "Irving" 71
In a Class All by Herself: "Myrt" 83
"Frances" 85
"Frank": The Fastest Fighter in Service with Japan's Air Forces 97
The Nakajima Ki-87: "Big Boy" 101
"Peggy" Arrived in Time to Be Too Late! 109
"Jacks" Are Better! 113
A "Jack" Is "Captured" by the 49th Fighter Group 121
The Last Roundup 127
Random Remarks 133

Postscript 139
New Material 141
About the Author by Harold A. Williams 156

FOREWORD

I am deeply indebted to Stackpole Books' history editor, Chris Evans, for allowing me the opportunity to offer a few comments, on what many consider to be one of the finest photo essays on Japanese aircraft. This book is regarded as a must have, whether you be an aircraft historian, enthusiast, or aircraft modeler such as myself. My initial exposure to James P. Gallagher's *Meatballs and Dead Birds* was back in the early 1970s, when I first viewed a friend's copy. If I could use only one word to describe my first reaction to the book, the word would be "covetous," which the Oxford Dictionary defines as "eagerly desirous of another's property." Based on my impression of the book and the opinions of others who either own or have read the book, the definition is more than apropos.

To date, there have been innumerable books published which offered many period photos of Japanese wartime aircraft; however, most suffered from the same deficiencies—namely poor quality photographs and sketchy, misleading captions. This is precisely what separates James Gallagher's *Meatballs and Dead Birds* from most other books, as photo coverage of the aircraft is clear and uncluttered and exudes a more casual pace, when time was plentiful and allowed for unhurried photography. All this, combined with firsthand commentary on each of the images, elevates this book to a standard that others could never hope to emulate.

As a child, I lived at a small, country airport that had many vintage aircraft in varying states of disrepair. My fascination with Japanese aircraft was piqued by the visit of a restored Aichi D3A Val dive-bomber to the airport where I was living and has continued unabated to this day. When I recollect back to those days, I can well remember playing in and around the wrecks and still recall the peacefulness that was so prevalent amongst all those silent warriors. I mention this because I get the same feeling when I look at the photos in *Meatballs and Dead Birds*. This book invokes a feeling that has not been obtained with any other book.

From an aircraft modeler's perspective, James Gallagher's photos are absolute treasures. He provides us with superb images of countless subjects, from the most common of Japanese fighters such as the Mitsubishi Zero, to the lesser known Nakajima Ki.87. The fact that many of the aircraft are photographed from both sides greatly increases the usefulness of this book from both a modeler's and historian's point of view. One could be excused for thinking that James Gallagher was himself a modeler, as his photographs, augmented by detailed captions, capture a level of detail which is considered essential for anyone who strives to build a more accurate model of wartime Japanese aircraft. The close-up photograph of a derelict Kawasaki Ki.61 Hein, accompanied by Gallagher's in-depth description is in my opinion, one of the most interesting subjects in the book, as he goes to great lengths to provide a most accurate description of this interesting bird. It is evident that he was certainly thinking of the model builder when he took many of these photographs.

Foreword

Of all the photographs contained within the covers of *Meatballs and Dead Birds*, the images that have the greatest impact on me are those of the huge junkyards of Japanese aircraft just before they were turned into scrap metal. These photos instill a great sadness in me, for they illustrate well the ultimate disposition of the majority of Japanese planes that survived the fighting. These noble aircraft fought for so long, only to endure the most humiliating defeat of all—to be pushed aside like old trash, never to be seen again. It is unfortunate that more Japanese aircraft were not preserved for future generations to view in museums. The destruction of these planes has only added to the importance of James Gallagher's photo essay, as these images, of necessity, now take the place of real examples on display in museums.

Regardless whether you call it foresight, or casual interest, we should consider ourselves fortunate that James Gallagher had an interest in photographing and documenting these airframes. No other publication so clearly documents the state of Imperial Japanese Army and Navy aircraft at this late stage of the war. Thank you, Mr. Gallagher, for preserving this piece of history.

Randy Lutz
July 2004

INTRODUCTION

*M*eatballs and Dead Birds. Is not this an odd title? Maybe so, then maybe not, but I'll wager that it attracted your attention . . . or else simply aroused your curiosity enough to take a second look at this book.

After much thought this title, which first struck me spontaneously, endured to the point where I had to get out my old (but I think well preserved) negatives of pictures from my overseas duty in World War II. I then sorted out my pics of Japanese aircraft and decided to do something about them. What you see here is the result of my work.

But back to the title—and here's why. During World War II in the Pacific against Japan, anyone who saw an enemy plane "anyway near close" would see also the bold red insignia representing the Rising Sun. Whether one be a flyer, ground crewman, in anti-aircraft defense, a soldier, engineer, Marine or Naval Personnel, just anybody, it made no difference, this insignia would simply be called a "meatball." For those of us who served in combat areas, what ground crewman has not heard, "hit it, that baby has meatballs!!"

I think that point is clear, but I do wonder how few, if any Americans out in the Pacific during the war, knew that this round, red marking we saw is properly called a Hinomaru? This word translates to "The Sun's Red Disc."

Now, those Japanese planes that were left after the cessation of hostilities, with but a minimal exception, were to be grounded aircraft. We, who were very close to this end of Japanese airpower and to the planes themselves, could not help but look at these objects as "dead birds."

So, is there a place for a book such as this one? I would like to think so—let's take a look into this reasoning.

Go to a "good" bookstore, or go to a hobby shop, and you will find many books on aviation—some pertaining to the history of flying, some to World War I, some between the wars, some on commercial aviation, and so on. More specifically, there will be some World War II books, but one thing is quite sure, there is only a very limited number of Japanese military aircraft books.

Through the years I have built a collection of publications concerning the war in the Pacific. I have found that there is a scarcity of Japanese aircraft photographs in general. What photos there are seem to fall into three basic categories. First, there are the so-called "captured" pictures, usually most interesting, but mostly of poor quality as far as clarity and reproduction are concerned. Second, there are a few photographs of abandoned Japanese aircraft mostly taken on Luzon in the Philippines, usually at Clark Field, or at airfields near Manila. Third, there are the "official" type of photos which portray Japanese planes with American insignia. These last named photo types are almost of a "clinical" quality photographically. They lack "feeling and flavor," having been taken during periods of official evaluation of captured craft during the war, or of Japanese planes taken over after the surrender and transported back to the United States for testing.

Incidentally, from one publication to another, one often sees the same photographs over and over, so this will bring us back to the question of a couple

xii   **Introduction**

of paragraphs ago, "Is there a place for a book like this?"

I think there is a spot for a set of photographs that takes a glimpse at the end of a great airpower—a look at some planes of the Japanese Air Forces, both the Army and Navy, as they were at the end.

What follows will not be a technical or statistical approach to anything, it will not by any means be all encompassing in scope, nor will it be the last word on a subject.

What I hope is that it will be, by word and picture, a small addition to the history of Japanese air power for all. I hope it will please the air buff in his quest for information and photos. I hope, too, that the many model builders will find some new details on Japanese aircraft of which they were previously unaware.

What this book will be is a group of photographs never before published. Also it will be exhibiting photos all taken by the author. In this book there will be some "hefty" size photos for your pleasure, something I frankly have not seen in any publication concerning Japanese aircraft. And lastly, it will be a personal look at many planes accompanied by personal comments—if I may say so, "I went amongst them" for a while. Now look with me at some of the things I saw.

James P. Gallagher

A Glance at the Pacific War

To search into the historical aspects of the Pacific War at great length would certainly be out of place here. It should be noted, however, that when the strength of the Japanese military forces burst forth into a succession of victories in the Pacific, an unexpectedly powerful air offensive led the way.

The air arm of Japan was composed of an Army Air Force and a Navy Air Force. While the planes of the Army operated from their airfields, planes of the Navy operated from a fleet of carriers as well as land bases. As the war against the United States began, the aircrews of the enemy of the East were highly trained and eminently capable, especially those of the carrier forces.

The early adventures of the Japanese military forces were dramatically fast and successful and the "Imperial Wild Eagles" dominated the skies of the Japanese areas of conquest. Their fighters and bombers ranged far and wide, so much so that in 1942 some military people thought that the Japanese were flying twin-engine bombers from aircraft carriers as a regular mode of operation.

American bombing and strafing, and then the souvenir hunters, have made a shambles of this "Zero." These photos were taken at Tacloban, Leyte, Philippine Islands, in November 1944. The P-38s being serviced in the background belong to the famous 49th Fighter Group.

Some GIs inspect a Nakajima Ki-49 Army bomber. Dubbed "Helen" by Allied forces, these remains were photographed at Nielson Field near the city of Manila in April of 1945. "Helens" were used in substantial numbers in the New Britain-New Guinea areas, and in larger numbers in the Philippines campaign, where many were expended on shipping attacks, often via the suicide route.

As the war continued and the forces of Japan fought on, a great turning point in their fortunes was to take place—this happened at the Battle of Midway. It was here that Japan met its first truly serious loss. Four Nipponese carriers went down under the assault of carrier planes of the United States Navy. The destruction of these four important ships was the measurable loss suffered by the enemy's military machine; yet it was the immeasurable loss that hurt the destiny of Japan in its war effort. It was the severe loss of crack aircrewmen and expert maintenance men, not to mention the airplanes that were lost to a watery grave.

In the long battle for Guadalcanal, flying forces of both Japan and the U.S. experienced heavy losses. In Eastern New Guinea the story was much the same. Not generally known is the severity of the loss of airmen, ground crews, and planes that took place in Japan's forces during the struggle for Rabaul on New Britain. So important to Japan's strategy was this base that they even dispatched planes from the carrier fleet to base there in a futile defense of that forward bastion. Here, Japanese aerial combat losses, combined with planes destroyed on the ground, mounted to an intolerable degree. By the end of February, 1944, remnants of Japanese airpower withdrew to the island of Truk. During this campaign, the balance in air strength had tipped to the Allied side.

From now on Japanese airpower in the Pacific would die little by little—the Wewak and Hollandia areas of New Guinea became graveyards for squadrons of Japanese planes. The waters around Truk and Saipan swallowed untold hundreds of enemy aircraft. The collision of American forces against those of Japan in the Philippines, and then at Okinawa, resulted in disastrous losses to Japanese airpower both in the air and on the ground. B-29 bombers flying from the Marianas were striking at production in Japan. Airpower of the Rising Sun was going into eclipse in the spring and early summer of 1945, as the island of Okinawa was being secured by the U.S. forces and then built into a great base.

By July of 1945, a great buildup of American forces was taking place in the forward bases. We, who

Most "Helens" were camouflaged for service among the tropical islands of the Pacific Ocean. This shows the pattern of an off-white and a jungle green. The bright red Hinomaru here looked like a good "bull's eye" for a fighter pilot's guns. We wondered how insecure the Japanese gunner must have felt in this rear cockpit when American planes approached.

Many Japanese airfields were well stocked with fighters and some bombers. Here at Atsugi Naval Air Station, near Tokyo, we see a sampling of some of the well over three hundred combat planes on hand. In this one corner of the field, we see a goodly supply of "Zekes," "Jacks," "Irvings," "Franceses," and "Judys." In the background, C-46s bring in supplies. Photo taken in September of 1945.

were in the Pacific, "knew" that big things were going to happen soon against Japan: we were getting ready for an assault on Japan proper. However, a dramatic change took place, which was a complete surprise to us all. An atomic bomb was dropped on Hiroshima on August 6, 1945. There would come about great changes in plans of war by both Japan and the Allied forces.

While the strength of the American Forces was greatly built up prior to the atomic bombing of Hiroshima, the Japanese were readying their forces for the anticipated landing assaults on the Home Islands. There was no effective Japanese naval power left to meet the combined American and British Fleets. There were still many Army divisions in readiness on the Japanese mainland, but the one great factor of effective opposition against the invasion forces was the air arm that still remained. Intelligence reports that we heard indicated that there were still several thousand planes with which to contend in the future operations against Japan proper.

After experiencing what had happened in the Philippines and to a larger degree the Kamikaze onslaught against the Allies at Okinawa, it did not take a G-2 genius to know that the Japanese were preserving the bulk of their remaining Air Forces for a final body smash against ships of the invasion forces before they reached the shores of the Japanese homeland.

This prospective bloody and grim confrontation never came about. Three days after Hiroshima another great bomb was released against Nagasaki. Even the Russians were getting into the act by their attacking of Japan's forces in Asia. The disdain with which the average American long-term serviceman of the Pacific war received this news of the Russian intervention against Japan is another story that I don't think has been told—yet this is not the place for that story.

On August 15, 1945, a cease fire went into effect between the combatants. So, now the Japanese Air Force was to die—not by a fierce series of relentless Kamikaze attacks against troop transports of a great invasion force, nor in a bloody blaze of glory against a formidable enemy. These airplanes would die in an ignominious way, destroyed by the hands of the American Occupation Forces at their home bases.

On August 19, a surrender delegation of Japanese arrived at Ie Shima, which is a small island lying off the northwest coast of Okinawa. There they transferred from their white-painted planes to an American C-54, thence taking off to Manila to negotiate the terms of surrender.

Finally, on August 28, 1945, an advance party of Americans, principally elements of the 11th Airborne Division, arrived by air at Atsugi Naval Air Station which is about 18 miles southwest of Tokyo. Just days later, other areas of Japan were occupied by American forces securing the peace after the formal surrender signing took place on the battleship *Missouri* on September 2. The occupying forces gave priority to destroying the air capabilities of Japanese military aircraft on the airfields of Japan.

I arrived with ground elements of the 49th Fighter Group (P-38 Lightnings) at Atsugi by way of LST at the port of Yokohama, just a few days after the surrender, having last been stationed on the Motobu Peninsula on the northwest coast of Okinawa. We, who were there, saw the death of the planes of Japan. The first phase was the simple disablement of the airworthiness of craft so that in any possible "revolt" these planes could not be used against the ships in the harbors of Japan. Then came the souvenir phase as the occupation became a secure fact. Radios and instruments and the like were taken. The last phase was the removal and destruction of "bodies" to make room for now arriving American air power at various fields.

Disabling of the Japanese planes was a first order of business for the initial Occupation Forces. After the war, I learned that a program had been initiated by the Japanese military leaders to keep the planes grounded by removal of the props of combat planes. This was done to prevent instances of possible attacks by some "diehard" fliers. The planes that were still airworthy were quickly disabled by the occupying forces by breaking control surfaces or windshields, as well as the slashing of tires. Here is a photo that was taken at Atsugi in September of 1945 that "tells the story."

The "Zero"

In my time I have seen many polls, rating many things—top football teams, top musical hits, favorite stars, best TV shows, you name them. Yet I do not recall ever seeing or hearing of a rating of the "top ten most famous types of aircraft ever manufactured." I will wager that any panel of "experts" who could be polled would have this particular airplane among them, no matter what country the panel came from or how many panels were checked. The plane that would appear on everybody's list is the unforgettable Japanese "Zero" of World War II.

Here is a fighter plane whose name has been used in the title of more than one book of wide circulation. Its fame in World War II was to reach every corner of the globe. It literally led the way from the attack on Pearl Harbor through all the conquests of the Rising Sun in the Pacific. It continued to serve throughout the war, even to the last days when it was often used as a "suicide" dive bomber off Okinawa and Japan. It also served on interceptor duty against the B-29s and to combat roving P-51s of the U.S. Army Air Forces over Japan, as well as carrier based Navy "Hellcats." On these last days it was considered outclassed, but there were still some flyers at the war's end who would give the edge more to the American pilots compared to the Japanese pilots, who were in short supply and short in training. In a sentence, the late model "Zero" in the hands of an experienced pilot was a weapon to be highly respected by any opposing pilot.

In the early phases of the war this Japanese Navy fighter plane was simply called the "Zero." As the war progressed it became known as the "Zeke." The explanation of these facts should be noted. When this aircraft was first accepted as a standard type of plane for mass production by the Imperial Navy in 1940 A.D., that year was the year 2600 on the Japanese calendar. This plane was then designated as A6M Type '0' Carrier Fighter—thus from the last digit of the year of acceptance the title of simply "Zero" was used by all the fighting forces in the Pacific War. It was designed by Mitsubishi although Nakajima also produced large numbers of this plane.

There came a definite need for simplification in naming the planes of Japan. Toward the end of 1942 the Materiel Section of the Directorate of Intelligence

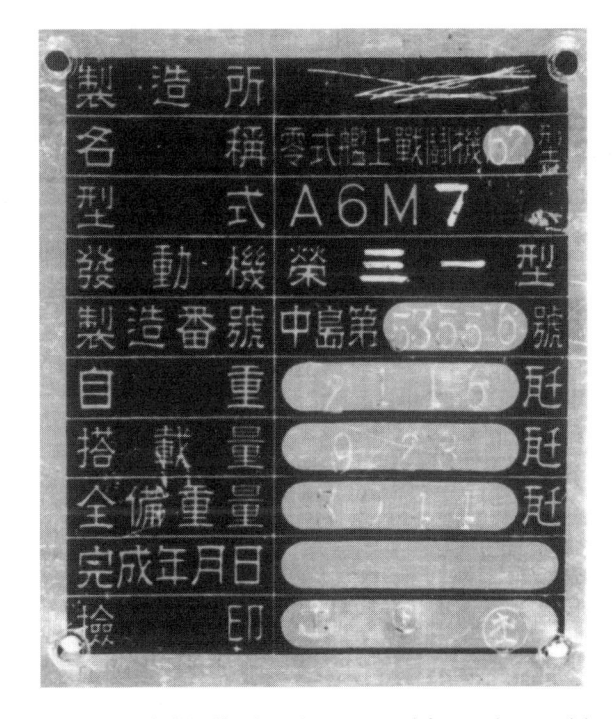

Manufacturer's identification plate removed from a late model "Zeke" that was based at Atsugi. Some symbols were blacked out, the 7 was hand marked with white paint.

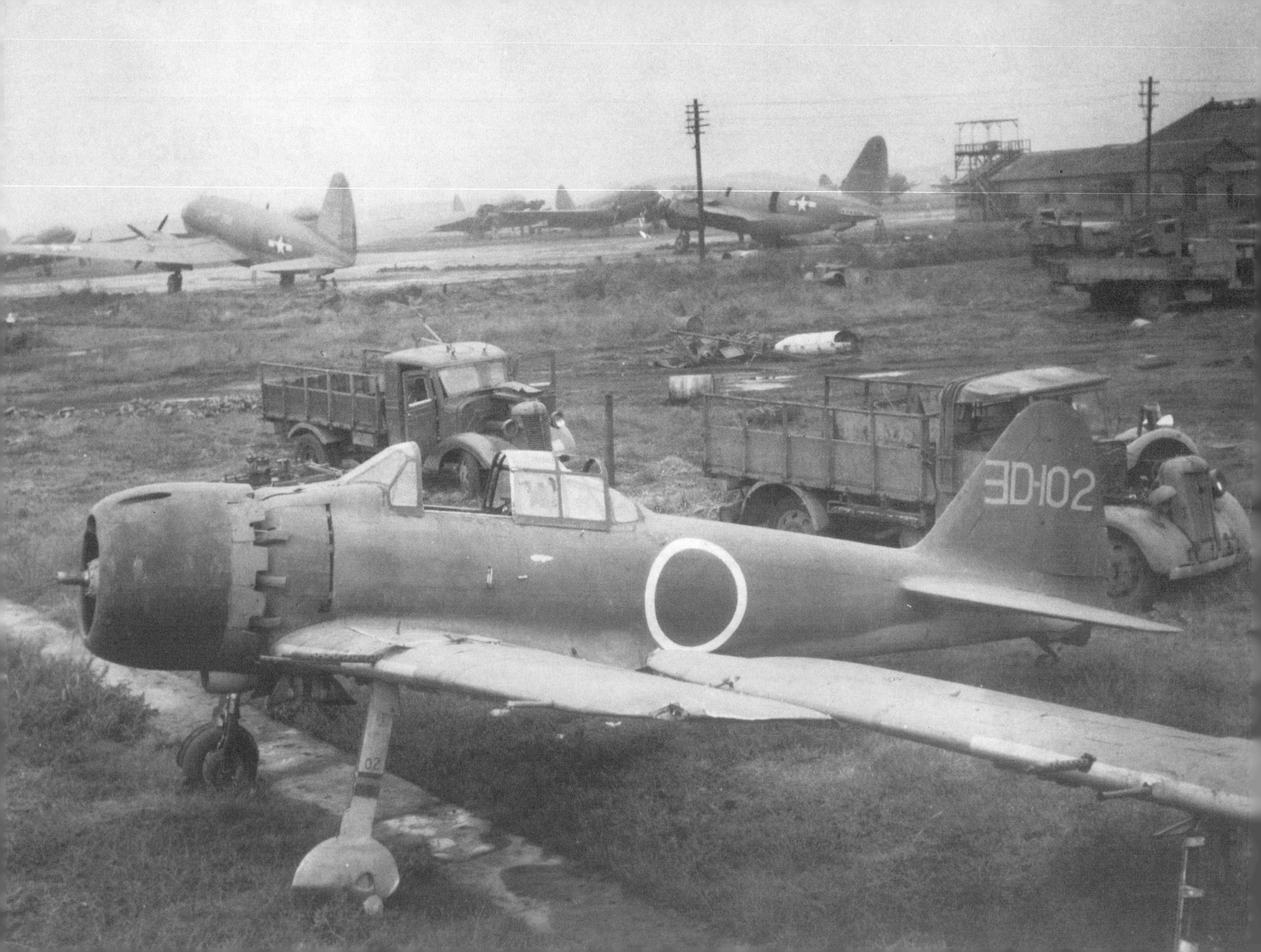
3D-102

initiated a standard "code" method of identification. Originally geared to the South West Pacific area of the Army Air Forces, by the start of 1943 however, this policy was accepted by all the Allied Forces against Japan.

Basically, the planes of Japan were identified by using the American names of males for fighter planes, female names for bomber types, and tree names for trainers. "Zeke" was the name "tagged" onto the "Zero" and when one heard fighter pilots talk of combat with this airplane after 1942, it was simply called "Zeke." In fact, we in the combat areas could recognize many types of aircraft of the enemy, but very few if any had the ability to "call" a plane from Japan by its manufacturer, title and type. All we knew was that "fighters had boys' names and bombers had girls' names," and what some of these names would identify.

Here are a few views of the famous "Zeke," and do take notice—for the first six months or so, this plane (in its earlier types) was Ruler of the Air in the Pacific War.

On the previous page, we view a late model "Zeke" at Atsugi. With the prop removed, this plane almost looks forlorn as it sits along the "sidelines" among some brushed-aside Japanese servicing trucks. In the background, Curtiss C-46 "Commandos" bring supplies to the early occupation forces in Japan. The building at the right of the picture is the operations building. The only "control tower" at that air base was a simple platform built upon the roof. As one of Japan's principal military air bases, it was surprising to the American forces just how few "luxuries" were there. For instance, the only substantial area of paving was one large all-weather strip of about 5000 feet, and a few small parking aprons. The rest was a dirt airfield from which operations were often carried out. Even most hangars had bare earth floors.

The photo above captures the classic beauty of this well armed "Zeke" fighter. This plane was painted a matte dark green on all upper areas with a dull gray-white finish on the undersurfaces.

The "Zeke's" principal claim to fame was its great maneuverability. In the hands of an expert pilot, it was considered the most maneuverable plane of World War II. This handsome plane sits among two "Irvings" and another "Zeke."

The late model "Zekes" in combat were armed with two cannons and four machine guns, some armor plate for the pilot, and had more horsepower. The American fighter planes facing them had the edge in technical quality with much quantitative superiority, and more thoroughly trained pilots. Though ready to fly, this "Zeke" never took off again—nor did its four brothers that are parked alongside it at Atsugi.

The "Zero"   11

In these two photos we see earlier "Zeros" with manually folding wingtips. This was done to allow them to be of short enough wingspan for lowering below decks on the elevators of Japanese aircraft carriers. Arrestor hooks are down below the tails of both craft.

Above, we see a covey of fighter planes. Some "Zekes" are mixed in with some of their younger and more rugged brothers from Mitsubishi. These are the "Jack," an interceptor fighter. We will take a good look at "Jack" a little later. We who were at Atsugi could observe that the older "Zeros" had been set aside either as trainers or as potential "suicide" craft, but that many latest model "Zekes" were ready to attack aircraft of their enemy. They were true fighter planes to the end of the war!

"Betty" the Bomber

There are two aircraft, which were used in Japan's air arsenal during World War II, that have gained aviation immortality. One is the famous "Zero" fighter which we have just seen and the other is the famous bomber which was to be given the name "Betty" by the Allied Forces in the Pacific.

This big two-engine bomber was the Mitsubishi G4M Type 1 Navy Attack Bomber. Like its stablemate the "Zero," this plane, with some modifications, was in service from the first days of the war until the end. In fact, what was probably the most important air mission of the war by Japan was the flight of two white-painted "Bettys."

The date was August 19, 1945 and the mission was to fly from Japan to the small island of Ie Shima, which lies off of the Northwest coast of Okinawa. This time it was not bombs or torpedoes that were the cargo, but instead a surrender delegation led by Lieut. General Torashiro Kawabe. Instead of being marked with the national symbols of Japan, the two "Bettys," freshly painted all white, had large green crosses. And notably the planes were not escorted by the usual "Zekes" but by a flight of United States Air Force P-38 "Lightnings" along with a lifeboat-carrying B-17 rescue plane. This obviously was a mission that must not fail—and gratefully it did not.

Earlier, there was another very famous flight of a pair of "Bettys"—April 18, 1943, to be exact. At this time things were not going well for Japan in the Solomon's area of the South Pacific. The Imperial Japanese Navy's "Number One Man" took it upon himself to make a personal inspection of the area to determine what military action should be taken, and also to bolster the fighting spirit of the Rising Sun's forces by personal exhortations.

However, Japan's operational military code had previously been broken and the exact timetable of the famous Admiral Isoroku Yamamoto's tour was known by the U.S. Military. A long distance intercept was carefully planned and executed. This time the escorts were "Zekes" and the attackers were P-38s flying out of Guadalcanal. An air battle took place near Bougainville and the "Lightning" fighters succeeded in shooting down the two "Bettys" as well as several enemy fighters. The Admiral's plane crashed on Bougainville killing him and his personal staff while the companion "Betty" went down into the sea, but sparing the lives of several aboard.

The completion of this now famous episode was not "celebrated" then, but was kept secret for many months thereafter, in order that in no way would the Japanese suspect that their top military code had been broken.

The largest in numbers of multi-engined planes produced by Japan in the war was this famous bomber. The "Betty" helped in the sinking of the great warships of the British Pacific Fleet, H.M.S. Prince of Wales and H.M.S. Repulse. These sinkings took place in the opening days of the Pacific War. Its use as a precision bomber in the Japanese attacks on the airfields of the Philippines caused decimation of American air strength there. The "Betty" became a feared plane, and it ranged so far and wide in the Pacific that for a time it was thought Japan was carrier-launching large bombers against the Allies.

When Japan lost the initiative in the Pacific, the vulnerability of the "Betty" began to tell, and the losses of this type of plane started to mount. The "Betty" was not at all capable of standing any "beating" whatsoever, and the loss of crack crews of airmen in combat reached telling proportions. Having been bombed by "Betty," it came as quite an experience to be able to personally inspect this famous plane at Atsugi. There were several there ranging from the earliest to the latest models. One of these was rigged for carrying the "Baka" bomb—a bomb which was actually a manned flying missile in which the pilot would attempt to fly into a ship. One was converted for transport duty. Others were various models of the standard bomber. Whatever the few improvements on this plane, you could hear, see, or feel the relative vulnerability of this craft by physical inspection.

The "Betty" had its good points—it could fly farther than a B-17 "Flying Fortress" and it was close to the B-25 "Mitchell" in speed. It was especially maneuverable for a large bomber, and it could carry a good load of bombs or a single large torpedo. But these favorable traits could not outweigh the lack of adequate crew protection nor the very poor protection for the huge fuel reservoirs aboard. By no means was the construction of the plane as rugged as were its American counterparts, and its combat losses became fierce.

Up to the end of the war a few "Bettys" were still being produced and some efforts were still being made to make the plane more combat-worthy, but by late 1944, the twin-engine "Frances" was coming into use and it was planned that this new and modern bomber would replace the "Betty" in the Imperial Navy's flying forces.

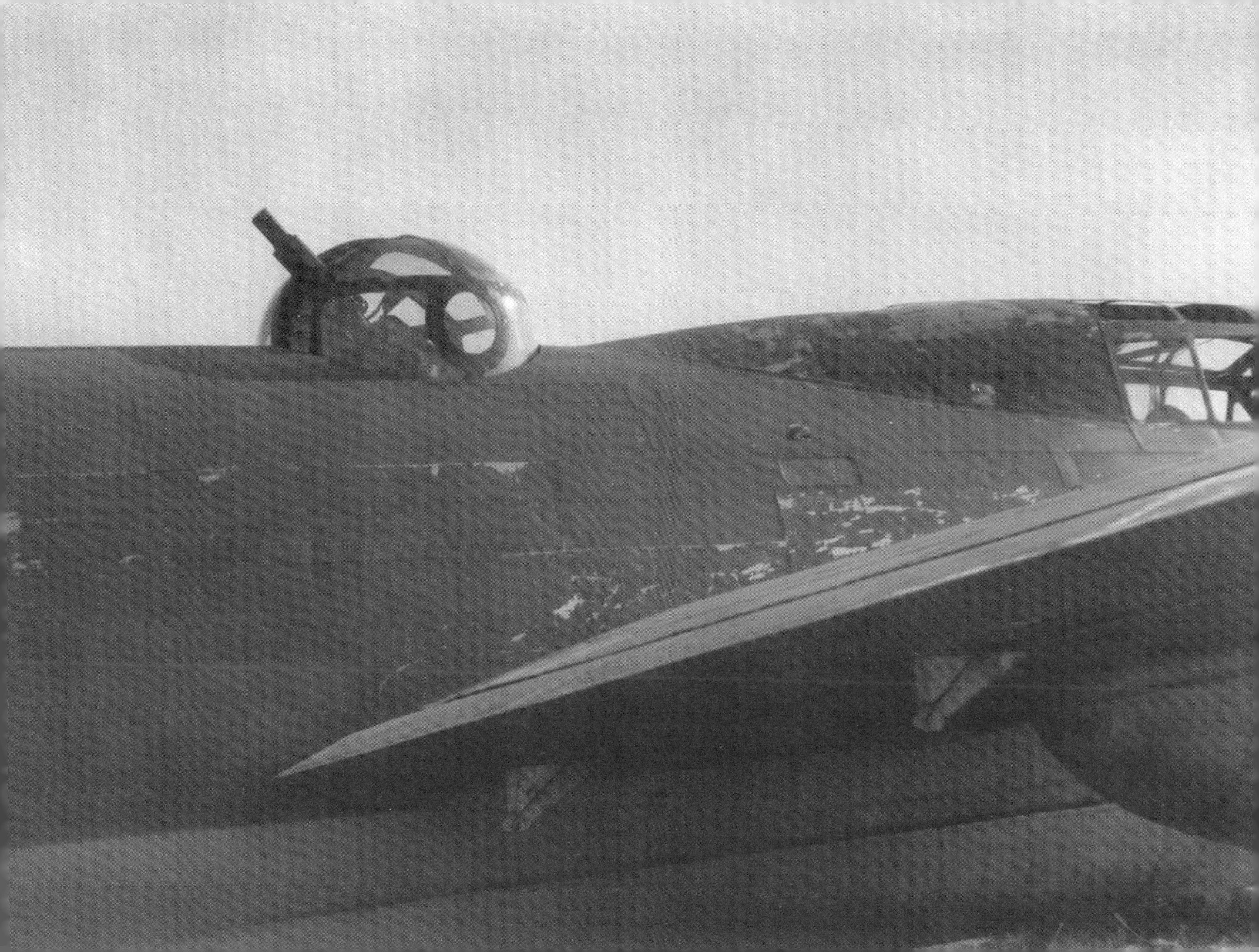

On the preceding page, we take a close-in look at a "Betty." The barrel has been removed from the 20mm cannon in the power turret. In the above photo, we see an older "Betty" that has literally been pushed aside. We do get an unusual view of this plane, however. The plane off the port wingtip is the remains of a "George," which was the only plane of this type at Atsugi. This late Japanese Navy fighter was conspicuous by its absence at this important air base, I thought.

"Betty" the Bomber 17

"Bettys" at Atsugi Naval Air Station, September 1945.

This plane was a "Betty." When the Japanese deemed it no longer of use for air duty, it then became a parts "depot" for other aircraft. Just about everything worthwhile in this plane had been put to use elsewhere, including the right aileron and the two engines. When it was no longer of any use as a spare parts facility, it was then put to use as a decoy. The idea was to spot this "plane" to draw enemy bombs and gunfire while carefully concealing good craft from view and thus causing the waste of ordnance. This particular one even had wooden paddles as props, now broken, and the cowl was held on by hemp to make the plane look "whole" from the air.

In the background from the left, there are the remains of a Japanese-held B-24 "Liberator," also a pilots' ready shack, and the upturned tail of a "Zeke" with the arrestor rod down. To the right of the picture are some P-38s of the 7th Squadron, 49th Fighter Group, resting on the airfield at Atsugi, September 1945.

B-29 Decoy

Here is a classic attraction. This wooden B-29 was set up in an open field adjoining the Japanese base at Irumagawa. Shortly after the war this base was to become known as Johnson Air Base, named after the great Pacific ace, Col. Gerald R. Johnson. We, who had a chance to examine closely this mock-up, concluded that it was planned and designed to attract American attack, while leaving the nearby base's hangars and planes as secondary targets. From the air it was to represent a camouflaged crash-landed B-29 which the Japanese must have felt that their enemy would endeavor to destroy, and thereby waste sorties and ordnance. However, there were no closeby bomb craters or bullet holes in this "crate" as evidence that it had drawn attack. This was taken in October of 1945.

During the war the Japanese used decoys and camouflage to some advantage. They were known to have set out a no longer serviceable plane in an attractive spot to draw strafing and in turn place concealed guns nearby to "trap" the enemy into heavy fire. Decoys of this type have been loaded with wired explosives to be set off in the face of low flying attacking enemy planes. Many times anti-aircraft gun positions were moved to new locations, while replacing the former guns with wooden imitations, in the hopes of avoiding direct air attack against the defensive weapons. In retrospect, there was surely a deadly game of "cat and mouse" going on.

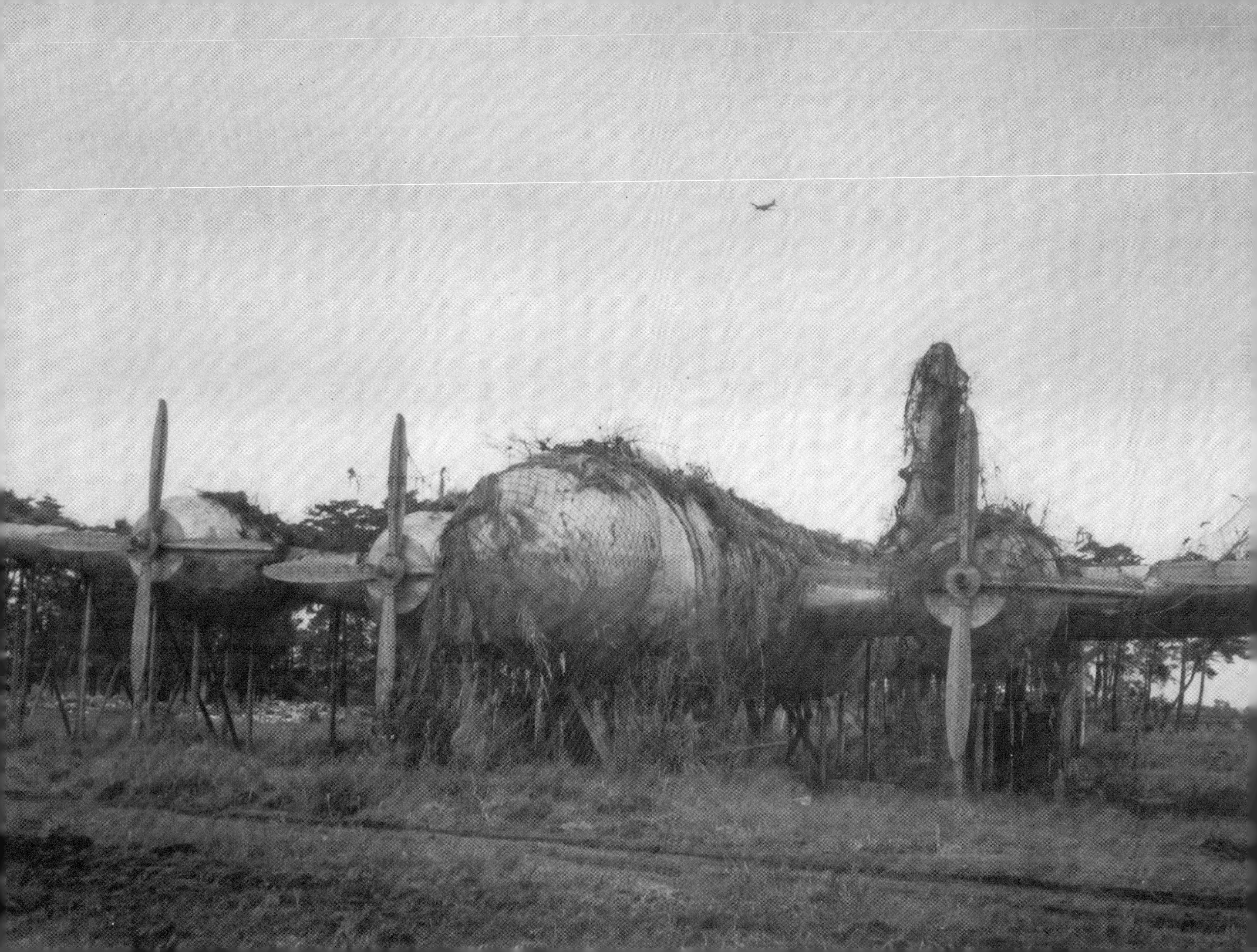

The Aichi D3A "Val"

When Pearl Harbor was struck on December 7, 1941, the attacking aircraft launched by the Japanese carriers were made up of three types of planes—the Mitsubishi A6M "Zero" Fighter, the Nakajima B5N "Kate," which was used both as a torpedo bomber and as a level bomber, and lastly, the Aichi D3A "Val" dive bomber, which type is pictured here.

In the early months of the war this fixed landing gear plane was flown by highly trained aircrews and inflicted a heavy toll on ships of the Allies. However, after six months of success, the "Val" started to meet its days of reckoning as the opposition's planes, always superior qualitatively, began to overwhelm it quantitatively. Its relative slowness and lack of defensive capabilities caused losses to be very heavy in planes and irreplaceable air crewmen. This happened especially in the Solomons' campaign in the Southwest Pacific area. A repeat performance of heavy losses took place in the battles over and around Leyte in the Philippines where the heavy firepower of Navy "Hellcats" and Air Force "Lightnings" would hit flights of "Vals" and cause them to "fall like flies."

Here we see a war-weary "Val" dive bomber—one of several that was still based at Atsugi at the end of the war. This particular craft had a splotchy green and white camouflage. From what I could observe, it probably served its last flying days as a training plane before suffering some damage by being caught on the ground by some low-level strafing and rocket attacks. Notice the holes in the aileron as well as those below the Hinomaru.

This phase of the war was the last time this plane served in first line duty, as they were even then being replaced by the fast and modern "Judy" dive bomber.

At the time of the Okinawa invasion in April of 1945, "Vals" were expended in Kamikaze attacks in large numbers although some were set aside for use as training planes.

I found it remarkable that this plane was not identified by the code name assigned, as were most Japanese planes, by most U.S. Army Air Force personnel—this one was always simply called an "Aichi."

The "Nell"

We take a brief look at the Mitsubishi G3M Navy Type 96 Bomber, called "Nell" by the Allied Forces in the Pacific. It was used extensively in the Sino-Japanese War, but its high mark in history is listed in its sinking of the H.M.S. *Repulse* and the H.M.S. *Prince of Wales* during the first week of the war in the Pacific. The "Betty" bomber has been given an "assist" in this action but it was the "Nell" that must get the major credit for the results of this feat.

These Japanese aircraft summarily disposed of the two great British warships by combining accurate high level bombings and aggressive low level torpedo attacks off of Malaya on December 10, 1941.

The "Nell" was used extensively during the early months of the war, particularly against Wake Island and American bases in the Philippine Islands. In the southeast areas of Asia and the Dutch East Indies the "Nell" also scored heavily in Japan's early triumphs. However, even during these days, it was in the process of being replaced by the more famous "Betty." By the arrival of 1943, the "Nell" was no longer serving in front line duty in the Pacific fighting. By this time the planes of this type that were still serviceable were used for training purposes, or converted for transport duty. Near the end of the war, in mid 1945, many of these old planes were even relegated to "decoy duty" around Japanese airbases.

I saw five "Nells" at Atsugi and interestingly, no two were painted alike. I also thought it remarkable that a bomber of this size did not have a bomb bay—all droppable ordnance was carried externally, whether a cargo of bombs or a torpedo.

The photo of the remains of this "Nell" on the following page, was taken in September of 1945 at the northern edge of the air field at Atsugi. This plane was painted a medium green on all exterior areas. It is noteworthy that there were no Hinomarus located on the upper wing surface although they were painted on the bottom of the wings.

The manufacturer's identification plate shown here was removed from this particular craft. With the aid of a magnifying glass, the engraved numbers in the "blank" areas become more apparent to the viewer.

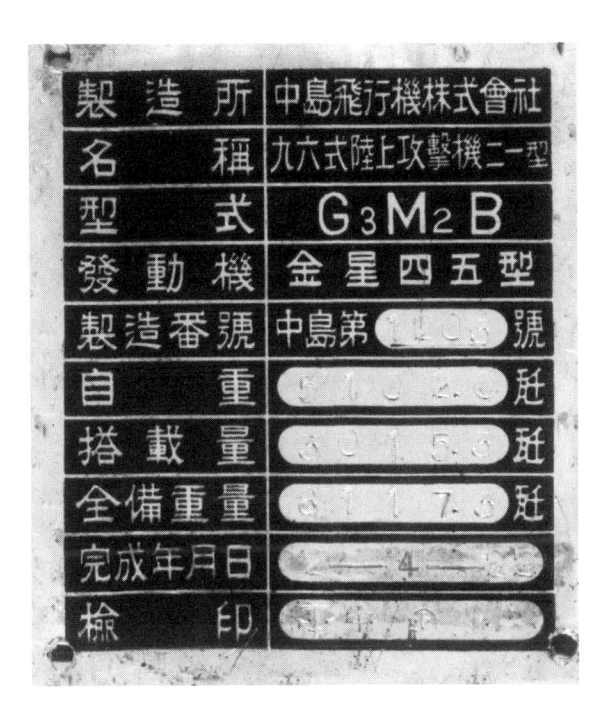

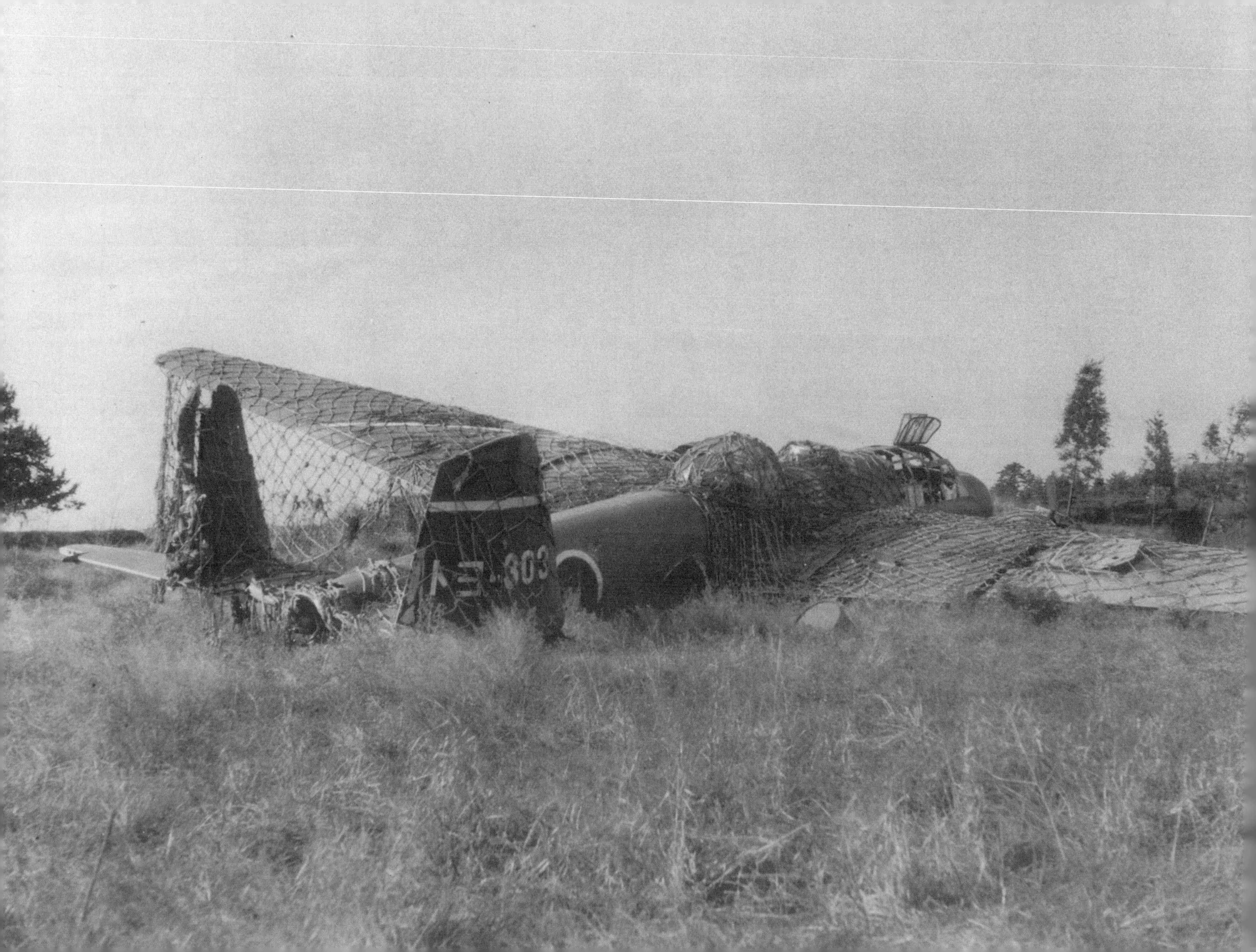
303

An Unforgettable Japanese Warbird

Having enjoyed the unusual opportunity of "inspecting" hundreds of Japanese military aircraft and/or their remains, I find that there is one particular combat plane that stands foremost in my memory. Here is a look at that plane, a "Tony" fighter.

Among American fighter pilots, the officers of higher rank and more particularly the aces, there was the "luxury" of assigned planes. This I know from my service in the Pacific as a Communications Officer with the 7th Fighter Squadron, 49th Fighter Group. These planes would be "decorated" with victory markings, and often, pictures of debatable artistic merit, or else, personally assigned names. This custom was not followed by the air forces of Japan. At any rate that is the impression that we had out in the Pacific Islands. The airplane was considered to be a weapon of war and not a personal vehicle of combat, nor a symbol of an individual pilot's glory. It is this fact that makes this particular "Tony" most noteworthy.

I never have been able to find out to whom this plane we see here belonged. It was a warbird that was certainly proud, possessing twelve B-29 victories and remaining undefeated in air combat.

Its color can best be described as a "chocolate bar" brown all over, and possessing brilliant red Hinomarus and, most remarkably, a large "Kelly-green" shamrock painted on both sides. This brightest-of-greens shamrock was bordered in white and located in front of the national markings on the sides of the plane. The vertical tail surface had the insignia of the 244th Sentai painted in white, and a five inch band of white around the fuselage in front of the tail surfaces.

The unforgettable plane that follows was photographed in September of 1945, at Chofu Army Air Base which is in the vicinity of Tokyo.

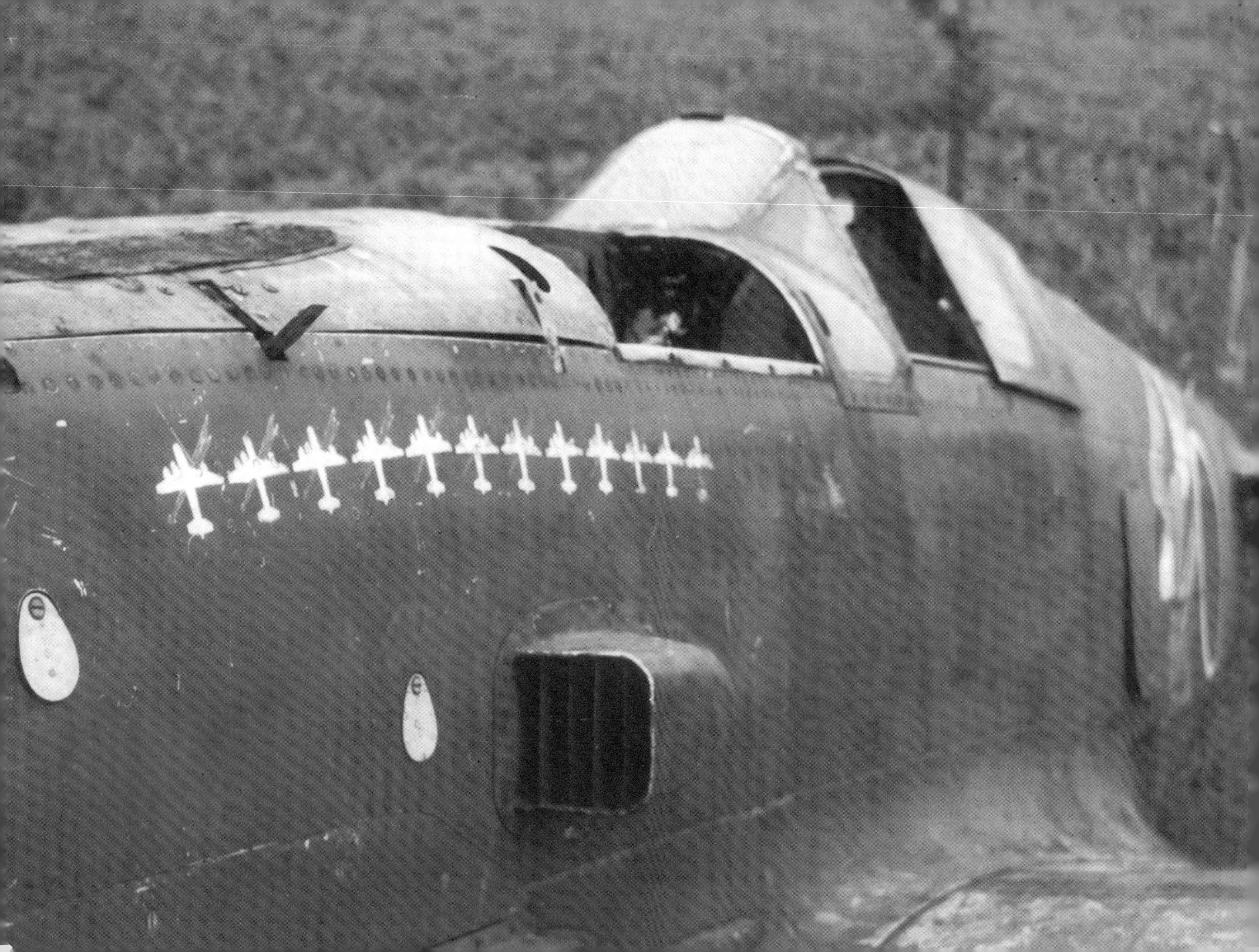

The "Dinah"

When the war opened in the Pacific, the Imperial Army Air Force had ready for immediate duty a substantial number of high-altitude reconnaissance planes. To the credit of the makers and the designers of this plane is the fact that, with just modest changes in design and engine horse-power, this aircraft type provided excellent service up to the last days of the war. This aircraft, called "Dinah" by the Allied Forces, was the Type 100 H. Q. Reconnaissance (Shin-Shitei) airplane manufactured by Mitsubishi.

The "Dinah" ranged all over the Pacific, where it gained, among the fighter pilots of the Allies, a great reputation for its high speed and elusiveness. In fact, there have been several times when I have heard P-38 "Lightning" pilots utter unprintable epithets of disgust after finally being directed by a radar intercept on a "Dinah" and then being unable to overtake that very swift plane. When an enemy airplane was spotted by the Japanese aircrew, the "Dinah" would "take leave of the place" and there was usually no catching up with this plane. Some "Dinahs" were reputed to exceed 400 miles per hour.

The "Dinah"

When on reconnaissance work the "Dinah" usually had no defensive armament, although sometimes the observer had a light machine gun—range, high speed, and elusiveness was the order of the day for this one. Near the end of the war some few "Dinahs" were modified for use as high altitude interceptors, but they came along too late to be used with any notable success.

This plane is considered, by many aviation authorities, to be the finest high altitude reconnaissance plane to serve in the Pacific War. Many of us who saw this plane felt it was the neatest and most beautiful in design to be used by the Japanese against their enemies.

The "Dinah" on the previous page was photographed at Irumagawa, Honshu, Japan in October 1945. This one was painted a dark brown on all surfaces, a color which I thought was unusual for this type. The Mitsubishi KI-46 "Dinah" was usually painted a gray or else a light blue, according to most pilot reports I heard during the war. Notice the very large gasoline tank behind the pilot's seat in this particular aircraft.

Dead "Lilys" of the Airfields

We see on this page the Kawasaki Ki-48 Army Type 99 Twin-engined Light Bomber (to this also could be added the model number)—with a name like this it becomes quite obvious why a simple designation had to come into being for the U.S. This plane was to be given the name "Lily" when code names came into usage by the Allied Forces.

The "Lily" was in service from the first days of the war, where it served in large numbers especially in the New Guinea area, up to the closing days when in smaller numbers it was used for night intruder duties over Okinawa, as well as Kamikaze sorties around this island.

When the Japanese made their move into the Dutch East Indies area and the New Guinea-New Britain areas, the Mitsubishi Bombers (later to be called "Nell" and "Betty") were identified readily. However, other planes were just called "twin-engined bombers" in official reports when they attacked some of the Allied bases in squadron strength. Many times these flights had a share of planes among them that later were to be called "Lilys."

During the war the "Lily" was improved by the use of more powerful engines, armor for crew protection, fuel tank protection, and heavier defensive weaponry. With these improvements there was little net help in performance compared with the earlier models, and by the middle of 1943 this plane could not "compete" favorably with the planes of its enemy. However, the "Lily's" ease of handling on take offs and landings, combined with its moderate speed and good cruising range made it ideal for night raiding work. It was used in this fashion with reasonable success especially in the area of New Guinea. When the Americans returned to the Philippines at Leyte in October of 1944, there was a substantial number of "Lilys" on Luzon, but the relatively poor performance of this plane limited its effective opposition to the now very powerful American Forces that were to recapture those islands.

Based on intelligence reports that I did hear in those days, combined with my conversations with American and Australian air crews, and also photos seen during and after the war, I personally think that the "Lily" has a record that has never been cited before. I now propose that the following should be put on record: "The 'Lily' bomber was the plane most destroyed or damaged on the ground, by enemy air action, in World War II in the Pacific theater."

Both planes pictured here were taken at Iruma-gawa on Honshu in October of 1945. One is painted a velvet black on all surfaces while the other (above) is a medium gray with two yellow bands and one red band circling the fuselage near the tail.

"Clipped Wings": "Ann" and "Sonia"

On the next page, we see a pair of forever grounded "Anns" that stand among their own broken wings at one of the edges of the airfield at Irumagawa. This photo was taken in October of 1945. The proper designation of this make of aircraft is Type 97 single-engine bomber Ki-30. It was another plane from Mitsubishi and most of its war service took place in the China theater.

"Ann" was equipped with a bomb bay and had crew facilities for the pilot and an observer-gunner. Considered obsolete at the time of Pearl Harbor, I have never heard nor seen reports of its combat use in the Pacific Islands after the time of the loss of the Philippines by the Americans in 1942. It is my calculated guess that prior to war's end these two "Anns" had been used for training purposes. They were painted in an off-white with a rich olive-green camouflage scheme; all of the bottom surfaces were painted an off-white.

As obsolete as "Ann" appeared and was, an only slightly younger and most similar in appearance plane was to see action in small numbers up until the cease fire—fixed landing gear, with spatted wheels and all. That latter plane was the Mitsubishi Type 99 assault-reconnaissance plane Ki-51 called "Sonia."

I was given some low-level combat photos taken in late '43 and early '44, and they show the presence of "Sonia" at Vunakanau near Rabaul, as well as at Dagua and But aerodromes on New Guinea. When I was stationed on Middelburg, a small island off the northernmost point of Western New Guinea, several separate moonlight strikes were made by three or four "Sonias" during late August of 1944. These planes were based on the Island of Ceram and they would stage out of Jefman on Western New Guinea. During one particular night's work they destroyed five P-38s and damaged several others. They also hit the island's jetty, breaching the fuel line and starting a good size fire there. The 33rd Fighter Control's radio transmitter shack took a near-hit, putting us off the air for ten hours. The "Sonias" had dropped daisy-cutters, bombs headed by a foot long detonating rod, causing the bomb to explode just above the ground, spraying steel fragments widely above the ground's level. What a "quaint" name the GIs devised for that death-dealing missile!

All of the "Sonias" left the area safely and I was to have the rather unique experience, next evening, of hearing Radio Tokyo describe this small scale (but successful) raid rather accurately on its regular evening news-propaganda broadcast.

I'll wager that the role of the infamous nuisance night raider of the many Pacific Islands, Washing Machine Charley, was played by the "Sonia" on more occasions than any other individual type of Japanese aircraft.

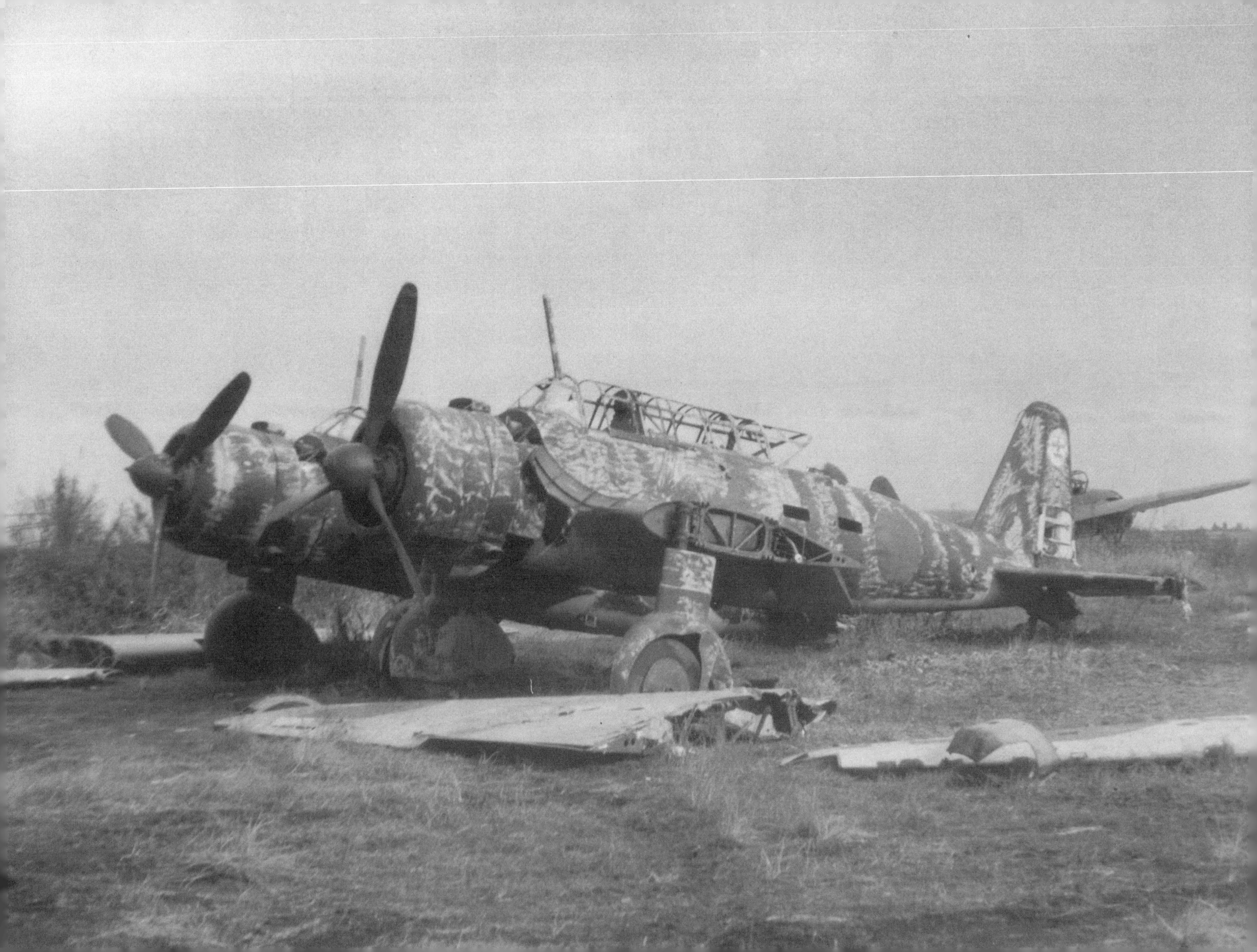

The "Tony"

The most often encountered Japanese types of fighter planes in the Pacific War were, first, the famous Navy "Zero" and, second, the Army plane, the Nakajima Ki-43 "Oscar." After these two types there was the only production Japanese fighter plane to be powered by a liquid cooled engine—it was the Kawasaki Ki-61 and named "Tony."

The "Tony" first appeared in combat in the New Guinea theater mainly in the vicinity of Wewak during early 1943. Its presence increased in quantity and in active combat as the year progressed. There were also reports of "Tony" interception missions against Allied raiding planes over and in the vicinity of Rabaul on New Britain Island. Although only relatively few in numbers there, that plane gained much respect from those who "tangled" with it. At Rabaul, the "Zeke" in various models bore the brunt of what was to end up being the futile air protection efforts of that once mighty Japanese bastion. While "Zeke" fighters of the Japanese Navy Air Force fought in the defense of Rabaul (most offensive strikes from that base, escorted by "Zekes," were undertaken by "Vals" and "Bettys" also of the Navy), to the west on Northeast New Guinea there was another great struggle going on. This contest of war matched the air capabilities of the Japanese Army Air Forces against the Allies throughout the eastern half of the island of New Guinea. Incidentally, New Guinea is the second largest island in the world.

There was little or no publicity reaching the U.S. regarding this head-on confrontation of air power, due mainly to the vastness of World War II and the relation of the European and North African campaigns to the "less important" Pacific theater of operations.

There in New Guinea, through 1942 and all the way into early 1944, the "Oscar" primarily was to take care of the fighter duties of the J.A.A.F. It faced mainly the Allied Bell P-39 "Airacobra" and the Curtiss P-40 "Kittyhawk" fighter planes. However, during the spring and summer of 1943 the "Tony" appeared in squadron numbers and with this, Japan had departed from the light and sharply maneuverable fighter planes for the first time at the front. The "Tony" was speedy and more rugged. Allied fighter pilots could no longer simply power-dive their craft (the P-39 and P-40) to safety when running into trouble in air combat. The "Tony" proved itself to be able to take punishment as well as to "dish it out."

However, as the number of "Tony" fighters was increasing in the combat areas, the American Fifth Air Force was moving in the powerful P-47 "Thunderbolt" and the swift P-38 "Lightning" fighters in good numbers. The very capable "Tony" was too late and too few to change the direction of the air war in that area.

Inasmuch as the "Tony" was first used in combat around Wewak on New Guinea, it would be appropriate here to make some comments on that very important enemy base. I flew over that Japanese held area (in an Australian Bristol "Beaufort" plane) and I would like to make an observation. When we read or hear about the Wewak Area, it should be noted that the Japanese built four major aerodromes in the general vicinity. However, these airbases were located some miles from one-another along the northern coast of New Guinea west of Madang. From the air they were somewhat similar in appearance. Each of the

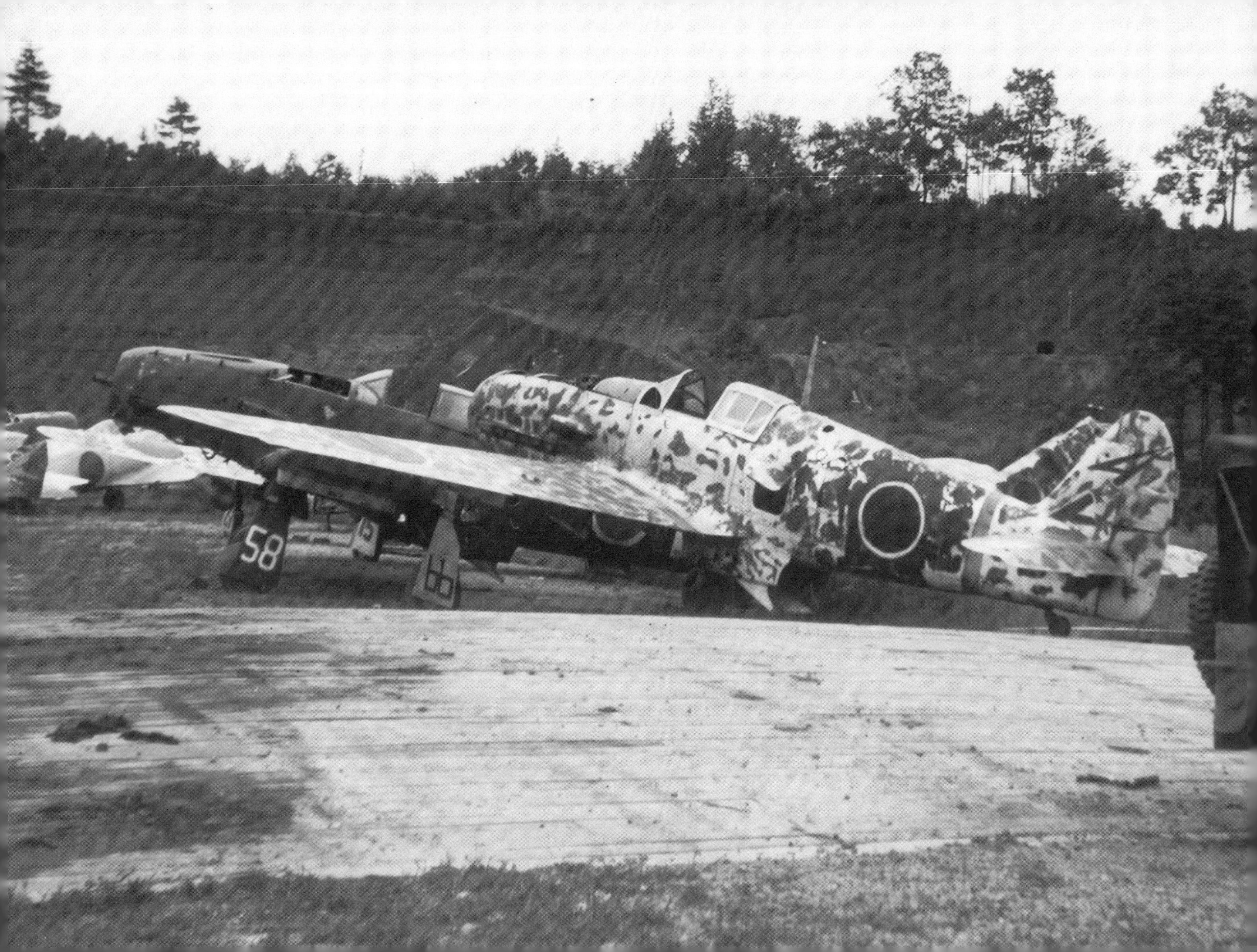
58
15

four stretched east and west in direction and were all located on a coastal plain which ran between the sea and mountainous jungle country. All were "dirt" airfields. The names of these aerodromes, in order going from east to west, were Boram, Wewak, Dagua and But.

When the power of the Allies, after a long vicious campaign, finally neutralized this complex of airbases in the early spring of 1944, the tempo of advance in New Guinea increased in a dramatic way. This western drive reached a successful conclusion with the landings in the Sansapor area, in late July of 1944. By this time, literally squadrons of Japanese aircraft, both fighters and bombers, were decimated or completely destroyed.

The handful of surviving "Tonys" was withdrawn to the Philippine Islands. Here, once again, large numbers of "Tonys" were encountered at and around Leyte in the last three months of 1944.

The tactics of offensive air power developed in neutralizing these very important New Guinea airbases of the enemy was something that the Japanese air forces could never equal at any time in the middle and late stages of the Pacific War. On some coordinated assaults on an enemy airfield, fighter escorted squadrons of B-24 "Liberator" bombers would open the attack by high level bombing of the landing field proper, rendering it inoperative, at least temporarily. The B-24s would also hit at anti-aircraft positions. This high-level strike was followed by low flying B-25 "Mitchells." Some few would take anti-aircraft positions as prime targets while others, flying at tree-top level and even lower, would rain para-frags, (small bombs with parachutes attached to enable the attacking plane to get clear of any explosions from their own bombs) on parked aircraft. A new word was coined for the successful air attack on the enemy's airfields, and this was used through the later stages of the Pacific War—a given Japanese airfield was said to be "wee-wacked"!

During the fierce campaign for Okinawa, in the spring months of 1945, the Japanese used in combat virtually every type of plane made within a decade of that tune—not only in combat in the usual sense, but also in "body-crashing" attacks against Allied ships. The "Tony" was no exception. However most of this type of fighter that remained on combat status were used as interceptor fighters for the Homeland Islands throughout the summer of 1945.

This almost bizarre looking "Tony" in the photo on the previous page was one of those that fought the American B-29s that were attacking Japan, as well as their escorting North American P-51 "Mustangs." The "Tony" also had to fight the roving carrier based Grumman F6F "Hellcats." Certainly this task was not an enviable one for any fighter plane to face, especially since the American planes were appearing over Japan in ever-increasing numbers.

This "Tony" was photographed at Chofu Army Air Base, which is near Tokyo, in September of 1945. It would have made a most exciting picture if taken in color. The base coats were a snowy white overpainted with blotches of olive-green all around the fuselage and on the upper wing and tail surfaces. The bottom of the wings and tail surfaces were all white. A six-inch bright yellow band circled the fuselage in front of the tail of the plane. The flashing thunderbolt on the tail was a flaming red to the first star, at which place it became a bright orange color. The number 66 at the wheels was painted black. When I took this photo I said to myself, "Here's one for the model builder!"

The pictures on the next page show two views of another "Tony" taken at Chofu Army Air Base in September of 1945. This particular base was one of those whose main job was the defense of the Tokyo area. At the end of hostilities Chofu was still very well stocked with many "Tony" and "Frank" fighters, as well as a few small twin-engine transports and a couple of what we called "Radial Tony" fighters.

In my readings after the war, I learned that many of these planes at Chofu belonged to what was probably the Homeland's most famous fighter group. It was the 244th Sentai (Fighter Group) and was identified by the flashing thunderbolt painted on the vertical tail surfaces.

Unlike the aircraft of most Japanese fliers, the "Tonys" of the 244th Sentai had many individualistic and rather flamboyant "paint jobs"—reminiscent of the Albatroses and Fokkers of a German Flying Circus in World War I that we had seen photos of and which we had read about the 1930s.

"Tony" No. 43 was painted an off-white base, on which was added medium green splotches of various shapes and sizes. The green splotches were on the upper surfaces of the wings and horizontal tail surfaces and all around the fuselage in the area behind the wing's trailing edge. The lower area of the front of the fuselage as well as the undersurfaces of the wings and tail were an off-white. The vertical tail surfaces were of the same red as the Hinomaru, with a bright yellow flashing thunderbolt unit marking. In front of the tail a tri-color band of yellow, white and red ringed the fuselage. An orange-red lightning streak ran from the nose to the cockpit, and the wings' lead-

36 The "Tony"

ing edges were painted yellow from the fuselage out to the underwing racks.

The "Tony" seen here was equipped with auxiliary fuel drop-tanks which were painted yellow. This added even more to what was a remarkably beautiful fighter plane.

As I look at these photos while writing this, I wonder about the "pride of ownership" of this particular "Tony": first, the pride of the Japanese fighter pilot to whom it belonged; second, of some air museum who might have owned this plane for display if it had not been destroyed; and third, of some pilot who might own this plane—and fly it now. Wouldn't it make a great attraction at an air show? At least I feasted my eyes one day, "inspected" the plane, and took the pictures that you see here.

A Touch of Americana in the Japanese Air Forces

On just first thought, by most people, the concept of "airpower" means an abundance of fighters, bombers and reconnaissance planes, all manned by trained airmen, and properly used militarily. But "airpower" needs at least another ingredient for totality, as the war in the Pacific was to prove—and that was the broad and at times the massive application of air transportation, both for men and cargo.

The way I look at it, this was one military element in which the Japanese were never to excel the United States in the war—not in quantity and not in quality. When Japan was in fullest production of planes for air transport use, these types of planes could be measured in hundreds while at this same time, in the U.S., their measure would be in the thousands. To boot, the U.S. was turning out highly trained air-crews for these planes that Japan could not expect to match.

Generally, the U.S. used air transport craft that were specifically designed for such purposes with the noteworthy exception of the B-24 Consolidated "Liberator" bomber. It was produced in large quantities in a transport version. Occasionally, American bomber types were pressed into air transport duties including some giant B-29s, but usually on a limited and temporary basis. With the Japanese Air Forces there was a different story. Lack of regular air transport craft forced the production, as well as conversion, of standard bomber craft for this type of duty—a compromise that endured through the war.

Air "experts" (and we who were simply interested in aircraft and aviation in general) before the Pacific War calculated that Japanese combat planes were, at best, copies of obsolete American and European types. What a false sense of security this was as we were soon to find out after Pearl Harbor! However, some of the Japanese transport planes were licensed copies of American craft, most notably of Douglas types, and they served from the first days of the war until its end, showing little quality improvement or new designs as did the Allies.

Some of the small number of transport planes which were to survive the war were retained, for a short period, in very limited use. These bore, in place of the Hinomarus, green "surrender crosses" and all flights, however few, were under strict control of the U.S. Forces.

Here we see a Japanese-built, should we say DC-3, or shall we say a Japanese C-47, or just call it a "Tabby"? At any rate, "Tabby" was the name assigned by the Allies to this "enemy" aircraft, a type of plane that was to serve the Rising Sun's Navy Air Force through the war in moderate numbers. It was that air arm's standard land-based transport and was used in both a cargo hauling model and also as a personnel transport.

During the late 1930s Japan had in airline service several "Made in America" DC-3s, and at about the same time started production of their own just slightly modified models for the military. Two Japanese manufacturers turned out the DC-3 type. The Nakajima company finished a few dozen of these planes, but the major producer was Showa.

The cargo transport model shown here was built by Showa. Note that there are additional windows in the flight compartment area as compared to the United States C-47 transport and the commercial DC-3 model.

37

When I first saw this particular plane I could not help but wonder just how many problems of recognition must have taken place during hostilities—and with what results. Taken at Atsugi in September 1945.

Here, and on the following page, we see three similar views of three dissimilar Japanese transport aircraft.

To the left is a look at the Mitsubishi MC-20 Transport which was known as "Topsy" by the Allies in the Pacific War. This was an adaptation of the Type 97 Heavy Bomber that was known as "Sally." Both of these types were used extensively, especially on the Asiatic Mainland, and also in substantial numbers in the Southwest Pacific area by the Japanese Army Air Forces. Besides the crew "Topsy" was equipped to carry a dozen troops. This photo of "Topsy" was taken at Chofu Army Air Base in September of 1945.

To the right, we see a rather rare plane. This large craft was originally produced as an attack bomber by Mitsubishi. It was the G5N1 Shinzan which meant Deep Mountain. Only about a half-dozen were produced, and when they did serve in the Japanese Navy Air Force, it was in the capacity of a transport plane. U.S. Intelligence could come up with only one photo of this craft as late as the December 1944 aircraft identification book. This was a vertical air view of one that had been blasted with a direct bomb hit on the ground and about the only thing identifiable were the wing tips. It was called "Liz" by the Allies.

Japan possessed only a very few land-based four-engine planes during WWII, although several four-engine seaplane models were used through the war in good numbers.

The "Liz" we see here at Atsugi was intact when the first occupation forces arrived in Japan. These early forces were only equipped with light bulldozers and tractors which were not powerful enough to remove this very heavy craft. This had to be done in order to make room for the Allied planes that were to be based at this airfield. Finally, a series of dynamite "jobs" blasted it into smaller and manageable pieces making it removable—the first of the series of "operations" had already taken place when this photo was taken. Incidentally, it should be noted here, the "Liz" was a rather loosely copied edition of the American Douglas DC-4 transport, the Japanese having purchased the prototype from Douglas.

Right, we see a very neat-looking twin-engine light transport built by Tachikawa. This plane was built in several models serving various purposes, a twin engine advanced trainer (some models were equipped with gun turrets), a land-based coastal patrol plane, a light bomber, and an eight-passenger military transport. Whatever the modification, the name "Hickory" was used. This transport version was photographed at Chofu Army Air Base.

Here was another instance where only color film would have captured the almost wild beauty of a particular airplane, but then, even a roll of black and white film was like gold in those days of scarcity.

Warbirds—Old and Retired

The two "planes" shown on this, and the next page, had both outlived their active service usefulness when these photos were taken at Atsugi in September, 1945. They had been relegated to use as instructional airframes, making their last service one of a training aid to ground crews. To the right was a "Claude," the Mitsubishi A5M Type 96 Carrier Fighter, which bore the brunt of Japanese Navy fighter duties in China before Pearl Harbor. It had been generally superseded by the famous "Zero" at the time of the outbreak of hostilities against the Allies in the Pacific area of operations. The "frame" in the next photo is a Nakajima E8N "Dave," a catapult-launched floatplane, used primarily for reconnaissance. This type was used by the Japanese in the first months of the war in the Pacific.

Upon seeing these "relics," they brought to my mind the old Boeing P-26 and the Vought "Corsair" of the mid-thirties—also before Pearl Harbor, most of us felt that "these were the kinds of planes we would have to contend with if the U.S. ever had any real trouble with Japan."

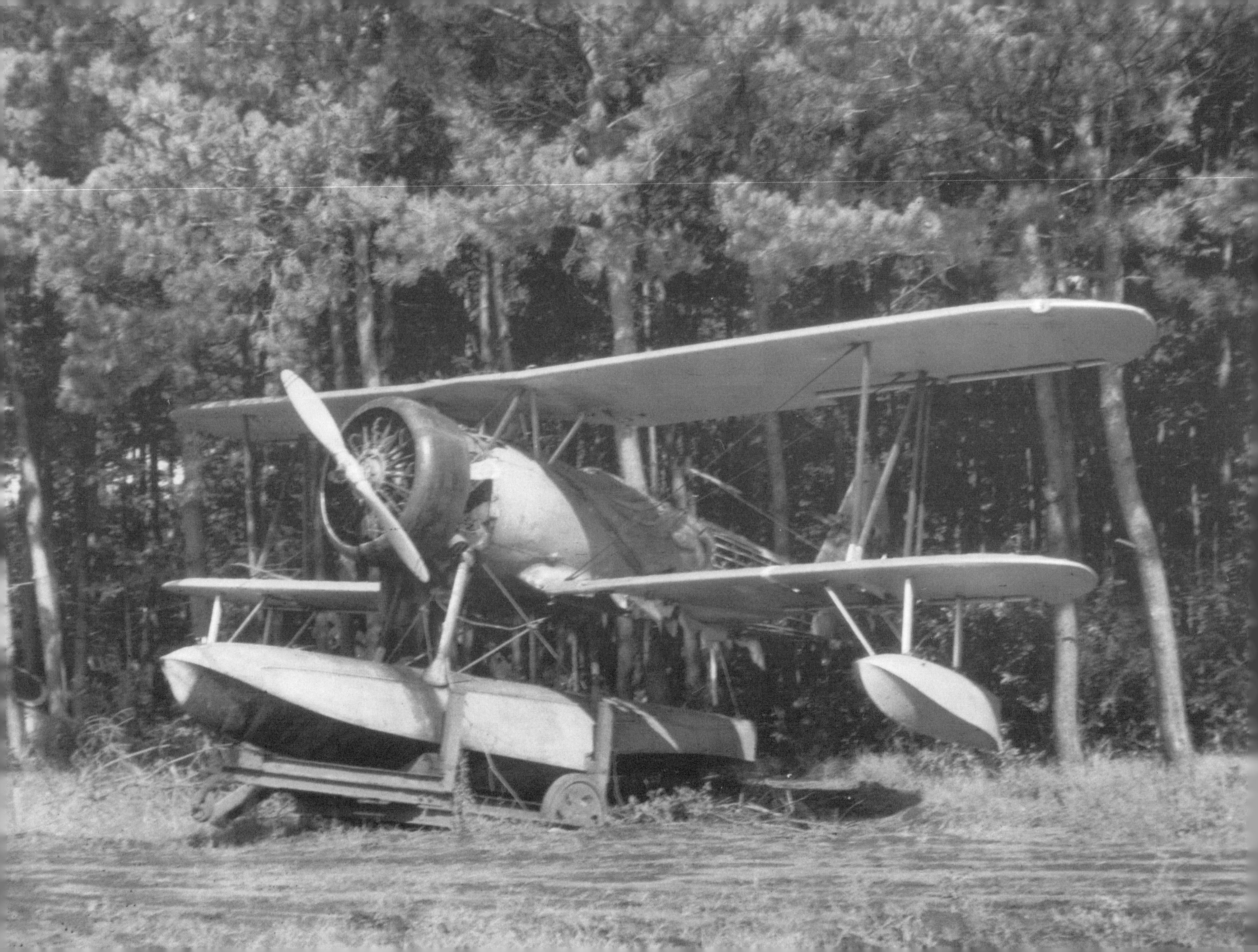

Warbirds—Lost and Found

When the Japanese military machine unleashed itself into a great sweep of the Pacific, immediately after the Pearl Harbor attack on December 7, 1941, its victories were stunningly fast and successful. The forces of Nippon rapidly took possession of the Dutch East Indies, as it was called then, and also swept easterly across New Guinea, New Britain, and the Solomon Islands, and even threatened a direct landing attack on the continent of Australia. The already existing military operations on the Asiatic Mainland were dramatically expanded. During these times, the Philippines were occupied, with the many important military bases built by the U.S. turned into offensive possessions of Japan. Other Pacific Islands, such as the British Gilbert Islands and the American outposts at Wake Island and Guam, were seized and turned into Japanese military bases. Japanese outposts were even established on North American soil on two of the Aleutian Islands off Alaska. These great military adventures were effected in little more than six short months—shocking events to experience then, and even now amazing facts to contemplate looking back in history.

The leading edge of this Samurai sword of conquest that cut such a great swath through the Asiatic and Pacific areas of our globe was the "Zero" fighter plane. One of this type of "lost and found" planes was probably the most noteworthy individual "find" of an aircraft during the Pacific war.

During the Japanese assaults against the Aleutians during June of 1942, which strikes paralleled the Midway attack, a Mitsubishi A6M2 "Zero," off a Japanese aircraft carrier, made a forced landing on Akutan Island. The pilot was killed in this emergency landing, but the plane itself was not seriously damaged. This important weapon was brought to the United States and restored to flying condition. This having been done, the "Zero" was put through extensive evaluation tests. Great returns resulted from these studies, leading to much improved U.S. fighter tactics to combat this very capable airplane more effectively.

In the early months of the war the Japanese forces were able to capture and test several types of aircraft of the Allied Forces, but none had such a noteworthy effect on combat operations as did this particular prize that was captured in the Aleutians. Among the several types of planes that the Japanese aviation experts were able to analyze at the time of these initial advances were the Douglas A-20 type (known by British and Australians as the "Boston" or DB-7B), the Curtiss P-40, the early Boeing B-17 "Flying Fortress," the F4F-3 (an early Grumman "Wildcat"), some Dutch-owned American made Brewster F3A's known as the "Buffalo," and the British made Hawker "Hurricane."

Whatever knowledge the Japanese intelligence divined from their tests, it must have proven quite valueless inasmuch as rapid and effective improvements of American combat planes rendered the captured war prizes rather quickly obsolete. Not only did the combat capabilities of American planes improve most rapidly but the quantity of these planes increased at an almost unbelievable rate.

In my rather extensive readings regarding the Pacific War, I have never been able to learn what later model U.S. planes the Japanese were able to "acquire" in any respectable condition after the end of the year 1942. In this regard, when I was stationed at Cape Gloucester, New Britain Island, in January of 1944 (which is at the opposite end of that island upon which was that great Japanese war base of Rabaul), we had the rumor concerning a certain American Consolidated B-24 "Liberator" bomber that the Japanese had recovered and would fly out of Rabaul. The Japanese were supposed to have kept this bomber carefully hidden from aerial observation and would occasionally employ it in either reconnaissance work or night assaults on American positions in the surrounding areas. This "myth" was never proven or disproven, but at least it was a notable conversation piece for us at The Cape through January, February, and into March of '44.

Speaking of Cape Gloucester, several virtually intact Japanese planes were captured by the invading U.S. Marines in December, 1943 at the airstrip there. I recall two particular planes that were carefully deck loaded on separate small coastal freighters for removal to rear areas for evaluation. This was done in January of 1944 and those "birds" were a "Tony" and a "Dinah," types of planes we have glanced at just a few pages back.

As the stalemate of the war was slowly broken during 1943, and the Allies in the Pacific started on the "long road to Tokyo," there were instances of recovery of Japanese military planes. In the Solomons, New Guinea, New Britain, and in the islands of the Central Pacific, the advances yielded some new "finds." However, nothing could approach the numerous Japanese aircraft found on Luzon in the Philippines, especially at Clark Field and at other airfields near Manila. The aircraft abandoned there by the retreating Japanese forces in the spring of 1945 read like a "Who's Who in Japanese Combat Planes," if there was such a thing. Many of these aircraft were in excellent condition, virtually ready for takeoff. Some of these were new types of planes, just released into

The photo above shows the fuselage of an export version of the American Douglas A-20. The identification plate shown here was taken from these remains. The British version was known as the "Boston," as this plate confirms, but it was noteworthy that the delivery date was omitted by the Royal Air Force. One might speculate that the British considered delivery dates restricted information.

The colors were the rather typical camouflage scheme used on many RAF planes through the years—an olive green used in conjunction with a mustard brown. It was weird seeing the red "meatball" upon this traditional paint job.

We who were at Atsugi, Japan, immediately after V-J Day and saw this "Boston III" could not help but wonder what long route this craft had taken and how did it end up as an instructional item for the Imperial Japanese Naval Air Force. How was it lost, and where was it found?

combat by Japan at the time of the American return to the Philippine Islands.

Much was learned from the evaluation of these planes that was to establish a new and high respect for the ability of Japan to produce some truly fine combat craft. However, these appraisals meant very little to the conduct of the war at this point. What if it was found that the Japanese had a fighter plane that was as fast as, or even faster than the great P-51 "Mustang," or what if still another fighter from Japan almost approached the rugged P-47 "Thunderbolt" in its combat abilities, or what if Japan was producing a plane that was in the process of being developed into a superior bomber interceptor. The answer was almost a so what? There was now an American (with other Allies) onslaught gathering tremendous power and momentum, sweeping in the direction of the Land of the Rising Sun with a force that was unstoppable.

The build up of strength that was taking place in manpower, equipment, and weapons of all kinds was such that the proper basing and deployment of all this might was becoming a real problem which was quickly solved by Japan's surrender.

Some things are simply American by nature, apple pie and the hotdog for example. During the war what could be more American than the Curtiss P-40 used by the U.S. Army Air Forces, even though many were "given" to some Allied nations?

Here we see a P-40 that was lost to the enemy but was found again by the victorious forces. As was done to most "enemy" aircraft, by the first occupation troops, this P-40 was also rendered incapable of ready flight by being intentionally damaged.

You can imagine what an incongruous sight this P-40 made to us few Army Air Force personnel who had the opportunity to view it first hand. It had belonged to the Japanese Navy for one thing—and for another it was very much out of uniform as it was "dressed" in the same green color as were the "Zeke," "Irving," and "Jack" Navy fighters of Japan that it stood among. And lastly, it was "decorated" with the red Hinomaru of its enemy—bad scene!

Let's discuss a little more about the Curtiss P-40 type in its relationship with the start of the end of the Air Forces of Japan. The story of its very successful service with the famous Flying Tigers in China is well known. Much less famous are its successes, as well as those of the Navy's F4F "Wildcat," in the early months of fighting in the Pacific Islands. It was mainly these

The then ubiquitous "Zero" never met the P-40 over Japan's home grounds in combat, but only in evaluation flights against captured planes. By January of 1945, the superb North American P-51 "Mustang" was replacing the P-40s of the Army Air Forces, although some of the latter still continued to serve through the Luzon campaign. However, when I later served on Okinawa, I saw no more P-40s—I do not believe that any were moved into that area by the Army Air Forces.

two fighter-types that had to bear the brunt of the attacking Japanese forces in the first year of the war. In performing this rugged duty they not only confronted, but slowly and surely defeated the very best trained and most capable pilots and air crews that Japan was ever to produce.

The "un-beautiful" F4F-4, a stubby and durable fighter, flown by Marine and Navy pilots from Henderson Field at Guadalcanal in the Solomons (as well as off carriers in surrounding waters) in late 1942 and early 1943, chopped away at attacking "Bettys," "Vals," and "Zeros." The "Wildcat" contributed a great deal to the stemming of the Japanese advances in that area. Farther west in New Guinea, flying out of Port Moresby and Milne Bay, the P-40 was being used by American and Australian fighter pilots. The P-40's mission there, as well as at Darwin in Northern Australia, was primarily one of defense during that critical year 1942—and that tough mission was to end favorably against the very best air attacks that Japan could muster.

Some historians consider the United States' landings at Leyte, Philippine Islands, on October 20, 1944, with its ensuing great sea and air battles, to be the climax of the Pacific War against Japan. I wonder how many, including avid air-buffs, know what were the types of planes to first be based on and to be operated from Leyte upon America's return. Well, the first planes were the Lockheed P-38 "Lightnings" of the 49th Fighter Group. Their ground crews (of which I was one) beached during the last day of the assault phase on October 24th. The P-38s flew in on October 27. Four days later five Northrop P-61 "Black Widow" night fighters of the 421st Night Fighter Squadron flew in and (along with the 49th) were based at the incomplete Tacloban strip. On November 3rd, P-40s of the 110th Tactical Reconnaissance Squadron reached Buri airstrip which was located about twenty miles south-southwest of Tacloban on Leyte. Once more the P-40 was in the thick of things!

The P-40 again went "up front," this time on Mindoro, which followed Leyte-Samar as the next major advance in the Philippines, and served there in the period of December-January. It is noteworthy that the Aussies fully used the P-40 on their move westward through the Dutch East Indies to the last day of the war.

Airfield Construction

Contributing greatly to the downfall of Japan's military adventures, and therefore to the end of their air-arm, was a "weapon" that has been relatively unheralded—that weapon was the bulldozer and its allies the road scraper, steam-shovel and other earth-moving and construction equipment.

There was no belittling the military capabilities of the enemy by those of us who were in the Pacific War, although here we earlier had cited the comparative weakness of Japan in relation to the U.S. in its air-transport qualities. However, at no time could Japan even touch the construction abilities of the Army Engineers and Navy Seabees in airfield and road building work, or dock construction and other essential projects. The American forces had the equipment and numerous experienced operators to build, and to do it fast—something the Japanese never did have, much to their detriment.

American construction gangs were able to put together an airfield, time being measurable by days, while an equivalent situation by the Japanese would be measured in weeks or even months. Thus, the island-hopping and coastal-jumping of the Allies was more than expedited by the great abilities of its "engineer" elements to lead the way on the route to Japan.

I have seen the U.S. construction men do their thing and also have seen reconnaissance and combat photos taken of Japanese airfields in the Pacific Islands showing some of their equipment—what a big difference! In fact, considering the lack of construction equipment by Japan's forces, it was rather amazing how well they did.

The expression "unsung hero" is certainly an old saw, but be that what it may, these construction guys have, to my knowledge, never been properly "brought to print"—maybe there is a cue here for a capable writer to pick this item up in its relation to the defeat of Japan.

And "Kate" Begot "Jill"

As the war in the Pacific continued, some combat planes had an almost natural sequence of development and yet these aircraft were to end up as entirely different models and therefore designated as such. Now, many things these days are referred to as second or third generation items, such as computers or jets for example, but in the days of World War II, the only "second generation" used was in reference to humans. However, in retrospect, there were a number of aircraft that could be called "second generation" types of planes. For example, there was the Grumman F6F "Hellcat" in relation to the F4F "Wildcat"; there was the Republic P-47 "Thunderbolt" in relation to the P-43 "Lancer"—there were others.

Here is one Japanese Navy plane that fits the designation of a "second generation" plane. It is the Nakajima B6N2 Navy Carrier Attack Bomber Tenzan (meaning Heavenly Mountain) and it was assigned

A "Jill" that was ready to fly—Atsugi, September, 1945.

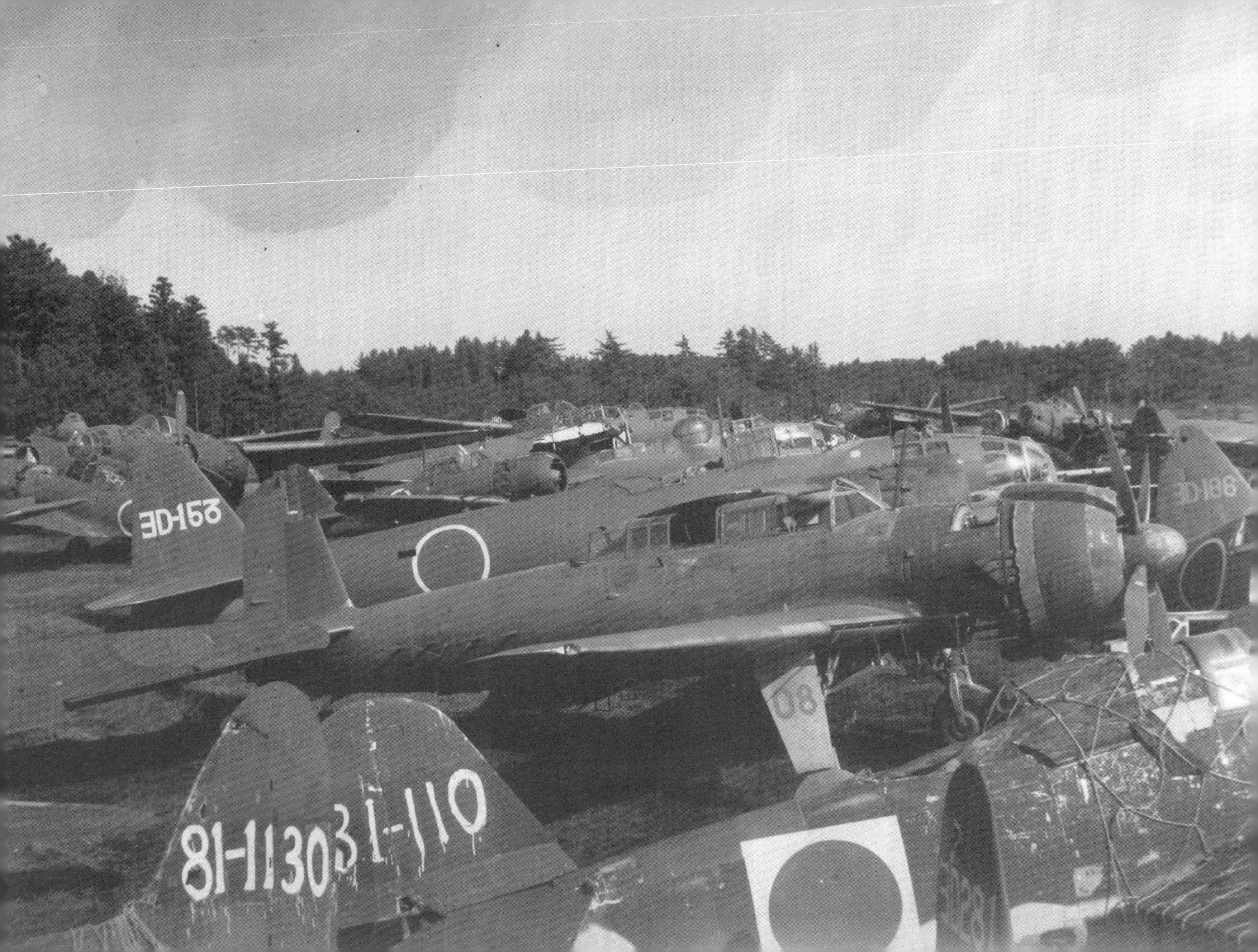

3D-153
3D-188
08
81-1130
31-110

the code name "Jill" by the Allies. Its famous predecessor was the Nakajima B5N2 "Kate" Carrier Attack Bomber, one of the three attacking types of planes used at Pearl Harbor (with the "Val" dive bomber and the "Zero" fighter). "Kate" served primarily as a torpedo plane during the early months of the war, and at that time had the reputation of being the best carrier-based torpedo bomber in the business. It also served as a level bomber at Pearl Harbor as well as during some of its later sorties against the Allies with good success. This was mainly attributable to its highly trained crews. In fact, the combo of "Zeke," "Val," and "Kate" was so successful, having Japan's best pilots aboard, that at one time the U.S. had only one fleet carrier on station in the Pacific, the rest having either been sunk or else docked under repair.

"Kate" was good but "Jill" was even better. "Jill's" horsepower was fully 75% more than was "Kate's," plus the fact that its operational range substantially exceeded the latter. A ventral gun position was incorporated into the "Jill," but it was still lightly armed by American standards. Unlike the U.S. torpedo bombers, there were no fixed forward guns used by the pilot to give the opposing gunners aboard ship reason to duck while under attack. Forward guns could, after release of ordnance, help considerably in fighting for the trip home with a now lighter, faster, and more maneuverable craft—but no such firepower was aboard "Jill."

Like many planes of Japanese design, the "Jill" was rated "a damn good-looking airplane" by the U.S. Army airmen and ground crews who had the opportunity to view her. Remarkably, "Jill" may have well been the fastest, farthest ranging, and most maneuverable torpedo bomber used by any power during the war.

"Jill" first appeared in mid 1944, and in increasing numbers later in that year around the Philippines and Formosa. In the spring of 1945, "Jill" reached the peak of its activity during the campaign for Okinawa. Although it was primarily designed for use as a carrier-based plane, Japan's severe losses in aircraft carriers caused most of "Jill's" missions to be flown from land bases.

I never personally knew of any army fighter pilot who had a "run-in" with the "Jill" and it looked like this plane was almost exclusively a Navy "Problem." What was wrong with "Jill?" I think the following: 1) too many F6F "Hellcats," 2) not enough "Jills" soon enough, 3) too many well trained sailors firing too many anti-aircraft guns from too many warships, 4) not enough fighter plane protection for combat loaded sorties, 5) too good U.S. Navy fighter-director teams, 6) not enough trained Japanese pilots, 7) too many F4U "Corsairs."

Among the literally hundreds of planes at Atsugi in September of 1945, belonging to the Imperial Japanese Navy up to the end of the war, there was only one "Jill" that remained at that airbase.

The "Jill" was very heavily expended in both conventional and suicide attacks against ships of the U.S. Navy—which brings up a thought. Considering the massive firepower of the Navy's warships that was used for anti-aircraft (some Navy vessels were virtually floating anti-aircraft platforms), a low level torpedo attack by Japanese planes, in the late stages of the war, was tantamount to a suicidal mission whatever the intent. This was assuming that a plane was even able to get by the Navy's radar-directed Combat Air Patrols. With all this opposition, I feel that by war's end there was only a handful of "Jills" that had survived.

Page 50 shows "Jill" 08, after it had been pushed aside. Good lighting here helps to bring out some of the details of this plane. It was radar equipped, indicating that it was one of the latest produced. The white band of the Hinomaru had been painted over with a dull green of the plane's color. There is no armor plate behind the pilot's seat—maybe it did not make any difference anyway.

The previous photo shows the "Jill" from still another angle, while the above one displays the rather rugged beauty of this big single engine torpedo bomber. It stands with a two-seat trainer version of the famous "Zero" fighter.

The "Radial Tony": A Plane with No Name?

Credit should be given to the air intelligence people in the Pacific during World War II for the beautiful job they did in gathering information regarding the military aircraft of Japan, and disseminating it to the U.S. Army and Navy units. I still have some of that material and it has been helpful in doing this work at hand.

Yet, there was one particular type of Japanese plane that was in active combat for several months that escaped positive identification by the Allies. We see on the right two photos of one of that type of fighter aircraft, taken at Chofu Army Air Base in September of 1945.

I remember well my first look at this particular aircraft. We went on a jeep tour, Capt. Ray Kopecky, Capt. Oliver Atchison, Capt. George "Doc" Webster and myself, from our base at Atsugi. We all were members of the 7th Fighter Squadron, 49th Fighter Group. At Chofu, we found that there were only three planes, out of a hundred or so there, that had been set aside for evaluation by the U.S. Military—this was one of them. It was obvious that this plane was not new, but on the contrary had apparently been in combat. Its olive drab color, with gray undersides, was weather beaten and glossless. The squadron markings on the tail had all but faded away. The Hinomaru was no longer a blood red but it had weathered into almost pink—this plane had been around for a good while

The "Radial Tony": A Plane with No Name?

and that was for sure, but what was it? Well, our decision was that it must be a radial engined "Tony," and this was so noted in my scrap book which I put together when I got home after my overseas duty.

Later, Japanese sources and American evaluation showed our appraisal to be correct. The Japanese in early 1945 had quantities of "Tony" airframes, but slow production of and troubles with inline engines had stalled completion of these sorely needed fighter planes. Experimental work was started by mounting radial engines on several of these fuselages and the trials bore fruit. This "hybrid" arrangement was so successful, resulting in a surprisingly fine fighter craft, that there evolved actual production of the "Radial Tony", which was known as the Ki-100 manufactured by Kawasaki. It proved to be the last production type of fighter to equip Japanese Army fighter squadrons of Japan in World War II.

When the "Radial Tony" was met in combat by B-29 crews or by roving American fighter pilots, it was often mistakenly called a "Frank" or "George" or else (correctly) an "unidentified fighter plane."

Several hundred of the "Radial Tonys" served and virtually all did so in the defense of the Home Islands through 1945 until the surrender.

The "Radial Tony" we see here has had its three-bladed prop removed, which does take something away from the good looks of the plane. A very large and well-rounded propeller-spinner was peculiar to this plane. This did give it a neat and streamlined appearance, not really apparent in the photos shown here.

Fighter Protection

Here we see some Japanese "fighter protection" in a different sense of the word than used in the conventional definition of the term. There were about ten of these highly protective revetments scattered at one corner of that very spacious area called Atsugi Naval Air Station. They were constructed of reinforced concrete, then topped with soil and sodded. A few had anti-aircraft gun emplacements on top, and at each there was an effort at camouflaging in varying degrees—some had hanging vines over the front openings, for example.

These photos rather graphically display how valuable first-line interceptor fighter planes had become as the war closed in on the Home Islands. This is not to imply that throughout the Pacific War the Japanese did not generally make the most of camouflage and dispersal to protect their planes on the ground. However, these "concrete hangars" seem to be Japan's last word on the subject. I feel that if it was not for the speed of the onslaught, there would have been much more of this type of aircraft dispersal and protection around Japan's homeland airfields. Yet, there was not enough time—another race which the enemy was to lose.

Upon inspection of these "concrete hangars," we figured that they were used not only for protective dispersal, but also as a safe place for maintenance and flight preparedness. They were so constructed that the openings in the back of each would allow the "running-up" of the engine so that a quick intercept could be started from a safe and ready disposition. The so-called safe hiding of these fighter planes reminds me of a little known fact that, to my knowledge, has never been mentioned in post-war writings. It is a rather small item, but one which I think is interesting. As late as March, April, and May of 1945, repeat 1945, Aussie ground troops in the area of the Gazelle Peninsula on New Britain were subject to occasional harassing attacks by a Japanese plane or planes. It or they, whichever, came out of the Rabaul area. To get the perspective of time, in April of 1945, Luzon was in the process of being secured, Okinawa had been

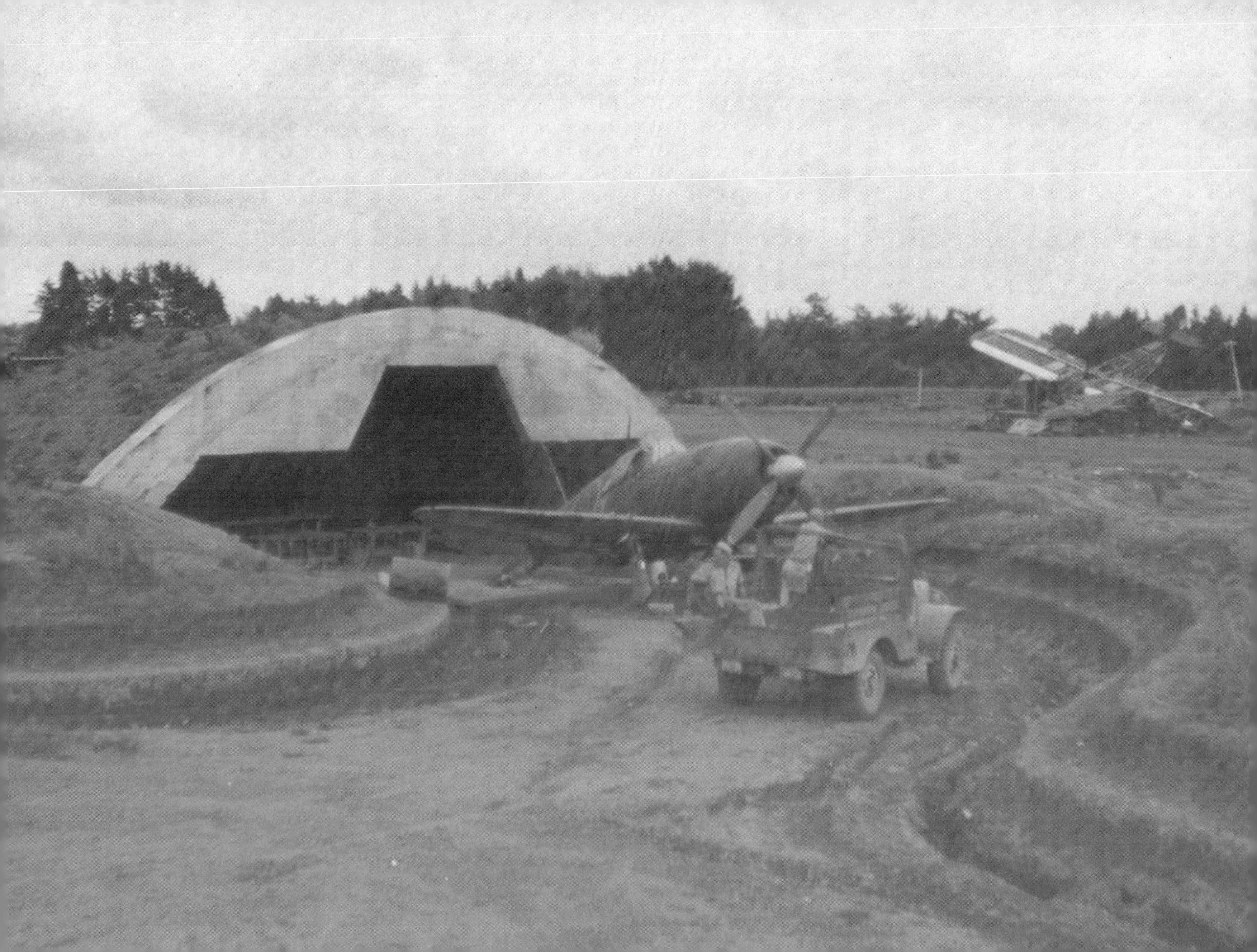

invaded, and Rabaul was a neutralized far-rear area. Nevertheless, the Japanese still had some good hiding places there for an operational plane or two.

Incidentally, my source of information on these raids was a booklet that was periodically printed and distributed to Army Air Force intelligence officers, down to squadron level. This publication kept the combat units constantly informed of the status of the enemy's airfields, available aircraft, roads, barge traffic, shipping, or anything about the enemy that would help in the war against Japan. During the war, this publication was marked CONFIDENTIAL—I always found it also INTERESTING.

It is my good fortune to have been given a batch of aerial photos taken during the Pacific War. Some show low level B-25 attacks, and others are reconnaissance photographs along with a few high level bombing scenes. They are very revealing regarding the ways and means of aircraft dispersal and protection used by the Japanese. Many of these photos were taken at what Japan called the "Southern Area" of operations, namely New Guinea, New Britain, and the Solomons.

At Vunakanau, one of Rabaul's four major airfields, there existed some of the best dispersal and protection seen at any base, Allied or Japanese, in forward combat areas. The Japanese had a concrete surfaced airstrip which was over 200 feet wide and 5000 feet long. Strategically laid out were 90 fighter and 60 bomber revetments. All of these were well scattered and most were well constructed for the parked airplanes' protection. Many had high built-up dirt walls and others were constructed of earthen blocks to a height of about 9 feet. (I would like to add a little "footnote" as to what the Intelligence people often called revetments as they noted them in marking reconnaissance photos. The dictionary says "a barricade against explosives;" the Intelligence guys said that these were "blast pens"—rather descriptive).

At the other Rabaul airfields a good effort was also made at dispersal and protection of aircraft. Also built were a few coconut log revetments, which were covered with earth and sodded, to serve as one plane hangars.

The major Japanese airfields at Eastern New Guinea, The Admiralties and New Britain had large dispersal areas and a moderate amount of revetments, but there was also added more effort at concealment from aerial observation. One method of disguising planes was to suspend bands of spaced cloth panels among posts, under which was parked an individual airplane with the hope of it blending into the ground when seen from the air. Some individual planes would be generously covered with palms and tree limbs while others would be literally tucked into the jungle.

Constant surveillance by Allied "Photo Joes" (as U.S. photo planes were called), and combat cameras mounted within attacking planes revealed just about everything that the Japanese were up to at their bases. Because of this, losses of grounded aircraft by the Japanese were extremely high. When squadrons of B-25s showered twenty-five-pound parachute bombs upon Japanese airfields in the Southwest Pacific area, and when the sharp shooting U.S. Navy fighter pilots in combination with accurate dive-bomber crews worked over the Central and Western Pacific areas, a tremendous number of enemy aircraft did not last long enough to get into actual combat.

One notable incident of destruction of grounded planes took place at Hollandia in Dutch New Guinea. In a series of strikes there by Fifth Air Force planes (with an assist from a carrier raid) starting March 30, 1944, over 340 Japanese planes were destroyed in just a few days. At the time of these attacks, the enemy wrongly thought that Hollandia was a safe distance from an effective daylight assault. Long range P-38s escorted B-24 high flying bombers, and then later, those fighters covered low flying B-25s and A-20s to work over the planes on the ground. The usual revetments were lacking, nor had there been any real efforts at concealment. Even aircraft dispersal was poor, and because of this the loss of planes by the Japanese Army Air Force at Hollandia was rapid and devastating. That air arm, after this airfield blitz, ceased to be an effective factor in the New Guinea theater.

The Incredible "Weapon": The Suicide Attack

With the advent of General Douglas MacArthur's much heralded "return" to the Philippines at Leyte—"A-Day" was October 20, 1944—a new type of warfare was introduced, although it was five days after the U.S. invasion when its impact was felt. On October 25, one U.S. escort carrier was sunk and three others severely damaged off the east coast of Leyte through intentional "body-crashing" attacks by bomb-carrying Japanese "Zeros."

Earlier during the Pacific War, there were isolated reports of planes intentionally crashing into ships of their enemy. This pertains to the actions of both the Japanese and Allied pilots. These crash tactics were usually attributed to the attacking aircraft being badly damaged or the pilot being seriously wounded by enemy fire, resulting in the flier spontaneously pressing his attack to the end. Now, a new horror was introduced into total war by the Japanese at Leyte, that would grow from a few volunteering air-warriors into an almost nationally sponsored military weapon. This was the planned and purposeful crashing of bomb-laden aircraft into ships of the Allies. The record

I was aboard the lead ship, an LST, of the last convoy of the assault phase at Leyte. On the morning of October 24, as we moved from Leyte Gulf into San Pedro Bay off Tacloban, the first major reaction from the Japanese against the US forces, on their return to the Philippines, took place. It was in the form of several air attacks, one of which approached the shipping off Tacloban with a force of some sixty planes. A big air battle ensued as US Navy fighters and ships' antiaircraft fire successfully contested this raid by the enemy. However, I saw two or three of these planes dive at nearby Liberty ships, barely missing them and I wondered then if they were trying to crash into those vessels. One very low-flying twin-engine Japanese bomber missed our LST (the convoy commodore was aboard) by about twenty-five feet, somehow hit a closeby minesweeper with a small bomb, setting the vessel on fire, and then deliberately plowed into an LCI. It was as if this small LCI was hit by a giant fire bomb, which this plane was tantamount to, having apparently an oversupply of gasoline rather than high explosives as cargo. The great battles for Letye Gulf and for Leyte itself had now commenced.

The Incredible "Weapon": The Suicide Attack

When I first saw the setting that you see here, it made a rather vivid impression on me. The day was a rainy, gloomy one in September 1945, at Atsugi—it was like visiting a grotto that was dedicated to death and destruction. Two of these manned flying bombs, carefully camouflaged and sheltered in sod-covered concrete, stood in readiness for a mission which they were never to make. This weapon was called "Ohka" by the Japanease, which in the English language means "cherry blossom." I think the implication here is that when the cherry blossom bursts into its fullest beauty, it quickly drops and dies—and so in the fullness of youth and manhood, when else could there be a better time to fight and die for the Emperor and the Homeland?

shows that "officially" the first international suicide attacks took place on October 25, 1944. I have often wondered if "unofficially" it was one day earlier.

The Japanese, as they expanded this type of attack, were to give the name Kamikaze to these pilots. Kamikaze meant Divine Wind in the language of Nippon. It was in the year 1281, according to a traditional story, that a great fleet of the conqueror Kublai Khan was approaching the Islands of Japan to effect a Mongolian invasion. A great storm struck, a Divine Wind, and wrecked the mighty armada of the Mongol warriors and saved Japan from conquest. Now centuries later, another enemy was pressing relentlessly, from the east this time, toward Japan. Another "miracle" was needed, and this was to be by way of the heroic pilots who would blunt the strength of the attacking fleets by means of body crashing assaults. These men, by their aerial banzai charges, were to mortally wound the enemy's fleets and thus save the Homeland—or so it was hoped. This often feared and always fierce Divine Wind could not stem the Pacific onslaught, but the word Kamikaze is one that will probably last forever in the languages of the world.

The highly successful initial attacks by a handful of bomb-laden "Zeros" were to bode no good for Allied men of the sea as well as for their ships, cargoes, and troops that they might have aboard. The Japanese leaders were certainly aware of the successes of these early Kamikaze attacks, relative to the conventional strikes, against ships of the U.S. Navy.

We, who were at Leyte, felt—as did the sons of Nippon—that these early crash attacks were not isolated instances but something that was bound to grow in usage—and so it did! It was to become like the infamous banzai charges of the Japanese infantry that usually came as a last-ditch effort at a given place when defeat became imminent. In late October of 1944, the airmen of Japan were starting to get into this grim act with volunteer Imperial Navy fliers leading the scene. They were soon to be followed by Army airmen cast in the same role of airborne guided missile pilots, as Japanese Kamikaze fliers might properly be called.

Through November, in the Leyte area, these suicide attacks were to continue in a sporadic way, often mixed in with conventional aerial attacks against ships of the U.S., but usually in sections of one to three aircraft. On December 7th of '44, when amphibious forces made their way to the Ormoc Bay area, on the west coast of Leyte, a new phase in Kamikaze attacks was to take place. There for the first time, several planes would swarm in an attack on a particular ship, unlike the previous individual efforts of the suicide-bent pilots. The Japanese by now had developed the Kamikaze concept into a major tactical weapon.

During the very important, but little known operations in the taking of Mindoro Island in the second half of December of 1944, and the subsequent landing on Luzon on January 9, 1945, the Kamikaze raids caused considerable damage to both warships and transports.

As fierce as these attacks had been in the Philippines, they would not equal the great attacks that the Kamikaze Special Attack Corps was to mount during the Allied campaign at and around Okinawa in the spring of 1945. Through the entire Philippines' campaigns, about 400 suicide aircraft were expended, sinking 16 ships and damaging 87 others. During the Okinawa campaign about four times as many aircraft were "one-wayed" against Allied ships, sinking 16 and, in addition, damaging 181. Also used at Okinawa, but with limited success, were the damnable piloted flying bombs, called "Baka" (fool or imbecile) by the Americans. These missiles were released from "Betty" bombers a dozen or so miles from the target. With the aid of three, small, solid-propellant rockets in the rear of the "craft," the pilot, the human guidance system, would make a controlled plunge into a "vessel of his choice," preferably an aircraft carrier.

Radar, in conjunction with the skillful direction of Navy fighter control teams, "steered" carrier Combat Air Patrols into early intercepts of the relatively slow "Bettys" carrying the "Baka" bomb. Fortunately, most of these sorties were intercepted long before the target areas were reached, and these heavily-laden "Bettys" became easy targets for the "Hellcats" and "Corsairs" of the U.S.N.

The suicidal efforts of the Banzai charge on land and the Kamikaze attacks in the skies had two counterparts at sea: the Kaiten (heaven shaker) human-guided submarine-torpedo and the Shinyo (bang boats) suicide boat. The Kaitens were released near the target from large submarines, while the Shinyos were shore based, from which they were to make their high speed contact-explosion runs against enemy transports. Unlike the actual as well as the psychological damage caused by the Kamikazes, the suicide-torpedoes and the surface crash-boats had minimal results.

In the last nine or ten months of the war the Kamikazes did do their thing. The damage inflicted upon the U.S. ships and those of its Allies was substantial and the loss of life aboard was severe. The suicide attack was symptomatic of futility, and of a final and dying effort by the air forces of Japan. It could not and did not stem nor even slow down the tide of defeat of the Rising Sun.

The question might be asked, "How did the men in the Pacific feel when the Japanese resorted to these aerial suicide attacks?" I think that the answer might be summed up in two words, "pretty bad!" Working on the premise that at many times in war, all men have certain fears or antipathies, I feel through my own experiences, and sharing thoughts with other servicemen with whom I was in contact at that time, that the Kamikaze attack concept was the ultimate in weapons psychology in the war. Certain varying degrees of tolerances seem to build up in most men against known risks of war actions, such as submarine attack, conventional air raids, artillery fire, and other weapons-use of the enemy—not that one becomes incapable of fear. The wholesale Kamikaze attacks were virtually incomprehensible to the minds of men of the western world. Some of the men felt it was that old last-ditch-stand philosophy that says, "If I've got to go, I am going to take along as many of you as I can." However, there was a lot more to it than that!

There were rumors floating around the combat areas of the Pacific in those 1944–45 days regarding the Kamikazes. Thinking back, possibly there was some kind of an escape or rationalization in these rumors to deprecate the absolute patriotism of the Japanese fliers. For one thing, the attacks were often dismissed as simply acts of fanatical self-destruction by the enemy. For another, the "word" was around that certain fliers were commanded to participate in this type of mission or be shot. Some were supposed to have been shackled to the controls of the aircraft—or else locked in the cockpit by sealing the plane's canopy so there was no getting out. It was also "presumed" that the Japanese Kamikaze pilots were so sakied-up that they did not care what would happen. Lurid tales like these were passed about, but were

Here is a closer view of the death-dealing "Baka" bomb, showing the cherry blossom insignia by the number 22. Apparent is the mounting lug (hook) in front of the cockpit that was used in securing it into the bomb bay of "Betty." As for the black line along the top, some of us felt that it was a sighting aid for its one and only dive. Also in the shelter are specially designed handling dollies for this weapon.

These "craft" were of wood and metal construction. The cockpits, possessing excellent vision characteristics, were equipped with rudder bar and stick, along with a couple of instruments such as compass and altimeter. There were levers to activate the rocket motors. Under the nose housing was a cannon-shell-like warhead of well over a ton. The span was a little over 16 feet and the length measured 20 feet.

quite lacking in fact, as we were to learn right after the war.

The men of the Allied Forces did not make use of the word "Kamikaze" until many weeks of this type of attack had passed. The average guy simply called them suicide planes, suiciders, or unprintables. The word "Kamikaze" started to become a by-word of "news" broadcasts, in the English language, from Radio Tokyo and Radio Saigon which were beamed to the Pacific areas. These broadcasts would tell of the exploits of, in their words, "The Kamikaze Special Attack Corps." Only occasionally would the descriptive words "body crashing attacks" be used. "Kamikaze" finally grew into American jargon by early 1945. However, I don't think that very many of us knew the derivation of that word. It was well after the war before I knew of the "Divine Wind" and its implication.

We were forbidden, in our letters, to mention or even suggest the fact that Japanese airmen were, at many times, resorting to crash-tactics or so-called suicide attacks. This was a no-no. Being for a period of time a squadron censor, I know that this regulation was strictly enforced up and down the line.

Some of my communications men would discuss and endeavor to determine the reasons for this rule, and I still remember a couple of the "answers." One sergeant-friend figured that "if it was not talked about and simply ignored, it might just go away." Another man suggested that we could not say anything about suicide attacks in our letters home because "it might discourage the folks back home." This was quickly rebutted by an "if it might discourage them, what the hell do you think it is going to do to us?" Maybe my sergeant-friend's humorous comment was not as unrealistic, on second thought, as it first appeared.

I do not recall, in my readings regarding the war against Japan, any discussion of military censorship in relation to the Japanese aerial suicide attacks. It was my impression then, and I find no reason to amend it now, that the damage to ships and the loss of men was so severe that the results of the Kamikazes was kept as hushed as possible—in fact, for a good period of time even the existence of suicide attacks was a military secret. This was done not to keep the peoples of the Allied Nations unaware of the results of these attacks, but primarily, as much as possible, to keep the enemy in the dark on just how successful—and serious—was the destruction wrought by these literally death-defying Japanese pilots. Simply stated, to report the facts of these successes to the world was an invitation for even more Kamikaze missions from the Japanese—and who in their right senses wanted more of this?

The Kamikaze attack—I said of this in November of 1944, and I'll say it again now—"what a helluva way to test the mettle of a man."

64 The Incredible "Weapon": The Suicide Attack

It was the Imperial Japanese Navy Air Force that initiated the planned suicide attacks, and that branch was the one that also employed the "Baka" bomb, the ultimate in WWII weapons of self-destruction. The Japanese Army Air Force was not to use a specifically designed suicide plane in actual attack because the war ended before the type craft we see here was generally released into combat service.

This plane was the Nakajima Ki-115 Tsurugi (Sword), of which about one hundred were built. There was no Allied codename for this one, inasmuch as it was not identified as a type up to the surrender of Japan. This plane was obviously designed and built for a one-way combat sortie. In the belly of the fuselage was a cavity for a large bomb. The landing gear looked like something that was put together in a plumber's shop—it was barely functional, having no shock absorbers, but having the wheels furnished with balloon tires to give some cushion to the plane upon take-off. The undercarriage was simply to be released from the wings after take-off on a suicide-attack mission. This particular Tsurugi was photographed at Chofu Army Air Base in September 1945.

Was There a "Favorite" Suicide Airplane in the Japanese Air Forces?

Before going ahead, let's take a look at a dictionary regarding the word "favorite." Used as a noun it is: 1. a) A person or thing liked or preferred above all others. b) A person especially indulged by a superior. 2. A contestant or competitor regarded as most likely to run. Now, used as an adjective it is: 1) Liked or preferred above all others. 2) Regarded with special favor. Passing lightly over the noun aspects, although grasping the ideas to an extent, it is the adjectival concepts that pertain more directly to the points that I would like to bring out.

While serving in the Army Air Forces during World War II, I did hear many discussions about the relative merits of the various aircraft used by the U.S. Military. There were classic debates regarding the merits of the P-38 "Lightning" vis-à-vis the P-51 "Mustang;" the relative merits of the B-25 "Mitchell" compared to those of the B-26 "Marauder" would divide some airmen into separate camps; the capabilities of the B-24 "Liberator" as opposed to the B-17 "Flying Fortress" made for two schools of thought. In the U.S. Navy there were divisions in respect for the merits of the F4U "Corsair" versus the F6F "Hellcat," as well as the SBD "Dauntless" over the SBC "Hell-diver." Not only did the aircrews have their say, but ground crews had their "favorites" as well as their dislikes too—and had plenty to say about it!

Certainly there was a certain pride regarding the capabilities of many of their own planes among the airmen of Japan. Some of the surviving Japanese fighter pilots expressed a great deal of respect for their aircraft. Many Japanese pilots considered their later model fighter planes to be equal, if not superior, to the American fighter craft.

It seems that little or nothing has been written by or about the personal feelings of Japanese bomber crews regarding how they felt about the aircraft they had to fly. They did not have such high regard for their craft—their losses in combat were fierce. This would be so because of their airplanes' inability to take any amount of beating, plus lack of sufficient defensive fire-power to fend off American interceptors. After all is said and done, one must wonder if the aircrews of Japan even had a favorite twin-engine bomber.

As the concept of the suicide attack developed into an accepted combat method and then was committed into wider usage there must have been a lot of soul-searching discussion on just how Japan's relatively depleted air power was to be exploited against the powerful approaching enemy.

Put yourself in the position of sitting in on some of those meetings of the Japanese "brass" as they considered how and when to use the aircraft and airmen of Japan against the mighty Allied forces, starting from the time of the U.S. landings at Leyte until it was all over. Imagine working out details on what squadrons of bombers would be committed to what suicide missions and when, or what fighter units would be expended in Kamikaze attacks, and what ones would be kept for use in the aerial defenses of the Homeland. Think about planning what existing aircraft to modify for more effective and practical Kamikaze attacks—consider, should you use the old "Vals" and "Kates" before using the fine "Judys" and "Jills" in this method of attack, or just mix them together on a given mission. Another thing to weigh

The "Judys" on these pages were all photographed at Atsugi in September or October 1945. "Judy" was built or modified for four basic uses: reconnaissance, dive-bombing, bomber interceptor and suicide attack. At one of the far corners of Atsugi, is seen the remains of a "Judy" that was used for B-29 interception. Note the angle of the obiquely mounted cannon in what was originally the rear cockpit.

Like the "Tony," "Judy" was manufactured with either an in line or a radial engine installed. On the next two pages are two photos of a "Judy" that was modified for suicide attack. There were no facilities for a rear crewman as was also the case with the plane seen above. There was no armament on this plane at all, but there was a large sheet of steel fitted behind the pilot for his protection (at least temporarily). There was also installed a bullet-proof windshield.

Remarkably, I have never seen another close-up photograph of this Japanese suicide aircraft. I feel sure that these models were heavily expended in one-way missions.

would be the question of whether there would be enough volunteers to mount large suicide—maybe some fliers would have to be "induced" to accept this kind of mission. Contrariwise, maybe there would be many more volunteers than there were airplanes available for attack.

To continue, should you husband your attack forces for the imminent landing assault on the Homeland by the Allied Forces? Would it be best to lash out at the enemy's warships and transports and try to wear them down before the final invasion fleet was assembled off the shores of Japan—or try to do a measure of both? Any way you look at it, the Japanese war leaders had their problems. While much has been written about the Kamikaze attacks from the Allied point of view, there has been but very little told from the Japanese side of the ledger regarding the last ditch efforts of the aerial suicide attacks. I think it should behoove some Japanese historian to publish an in-depth study on the subject of the Kamikaze operations. It would make a most important and interesting document, and I hope it will be started before the first hand knowledge of the events of those dramatic times will be washed away by the moving tide of time.

I feel that we may reasonably conjecture, from the receiving end as it were, as to what was (or were) the "favorite" suicide attack aircraft in the Japanese arsenal as selected by their leaders. Of any given type it was probably the "Zeke" that made the most attacks, due mainly to the large numbers available relative to

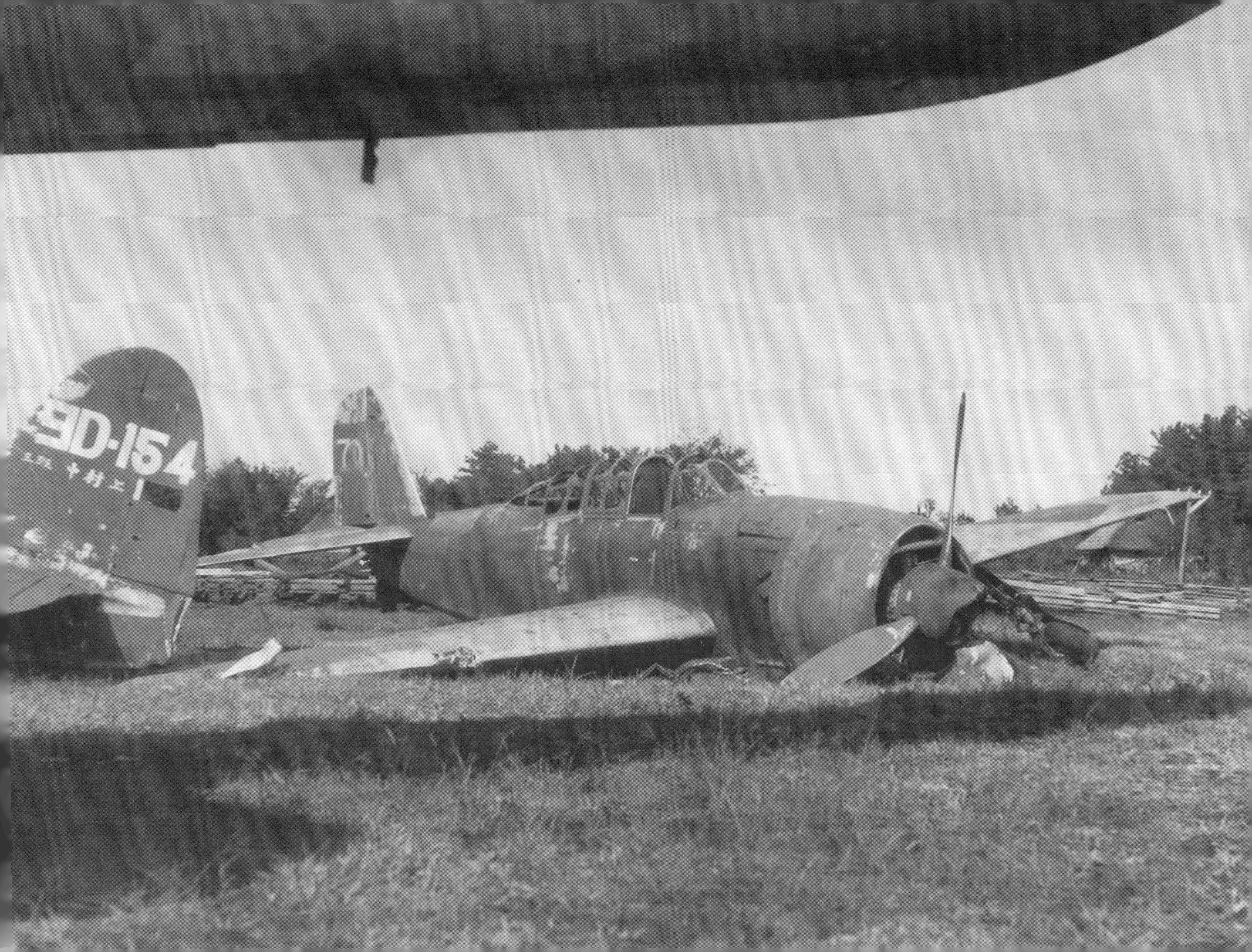
3D-154
70

other Japanese aircraft types. Also there is the fact that "Zeke" had wide distribution on the war fronts. It could be noted here, that with the start of the suicide missions around the Philippines, the type of aircraft employed was usually dictated by the simple factor of availability. However, commencing with the Allied operations around Okinawa, somewhat of a different pattern in aircraft usage became apparent. After the early phases of the critical Okinawa campaign, first line fighter planes were not too often used in crashing attacks upon ships, being generally relegated to Homeland air defense duty. However, many older "Zekes," "Oscars," and some war-weary "Tonys" were continually expended against ships. During the spring of '45, "Vals" were used by the numbers as were the "Sonias," "Peggys," "Jills," and most anything that the Japanese could muster from the airfields of the Home Islands.

I think that one particular Japanese plane type must stand out among the others as a "favorite" suicide plane. It could be the Japanese Navy's Yokosuka D4Y Suisei (Comet), called "Judy" by the Allies. It had earlier proven to be a versatile aircraft and was generally rated as being the fastest shipboard dive bomber used in combat in World War II. History tells us that a couple of "Judys" were available as carrier based reconnaissance planes by the Imperial Navy

These, and the two on the next page, are what I believe to be rather rare photos showing the details of the rear cannon mounting of a "Judy."

The "Judy" was a handsome plane to see. Dimensionally, it was but little larger in size than the standard Japanese fighters. This warplane possessed remarkable speeds in all its models but was severely short on protection of crew and fuel supply. The dive bomber version was capable of carrying internally a large bomb, while wing racks were installed to handle smaller ordnance. The "Judy" we see here and on the opposite page was built as the dive bomber version. The bomb bay doors are apparent as are the wing racks and the positions of the two forward firing fuselage machine guns. Some time later, this particular plane was fitted with an obliquely firing 20mm cannon within its rear cockpit, thereby giving this plane the rather unique characteristics of being an interceptor-bomber and not just a bomber interceptor—think about that for a minute.

during the Midway operations. Its use as a dive bomber was the first claim to fame, yet its lasting reputation will be that of being a feare d suicide plane. The fact remains, however, that it was a craft of such good performance that a number of them were modified for use as interceptors against B-29 attacks, especially against nocturnal raiders.

While "Zeke" flew the largest number of suicide sorties of any Japanese plane type, there is yet another way where one might speculate as to what was the "favorite" suicide plane of the military leaders. This would be the measure of the number of suicide sorties flown in relation to the quantity of a given aircraft type that was produced—and this is where "Judy" came in. It is my calculated opinion that this type flew more suicide missions than any other standard Japanese aircraft relative to the number of airplanes of a given type that was manufactured. A bit of credence may be added to this thought that "Judy" was "liked or preferred above all others; regarded with special favor." A relatively large number of this airplane was modified and produced as strictly "special attack" bombers.

Undoubtedly there was a good share of hassling among the Japanese powers-that-be about whether to resort to body-crashing attacks or not, what planes to use and when, and so forth. But in my view there is one thing sure: there was not much choice of aircraft type for use by the Kamikaze crews on their missions. Now, even if there was a pick of planes, I would liken it to having a choice of coffins for one's dying self.

Variations on a Plane by Nakajima: "Irving"

So far, this book has looked at quite a few distinct types of Japanese aircraft. Now, I would like to project the Nakajima "Irving" a little differently. I think that what is here may well be the "closest look" most buffs have had in any publication of this particular aircraft.

Besides telling what I saw, showing some of the things I have photographed, along with mentioning some things I have gathered from my readings, there will be a little more added.

By December of 1944, Air Intelligence had accumulated a fair share of the data on "Irving"—in more modern jargon they pretty well had the book on "Irving." In these pages there will be reproduced what was known about this plane at the end of the year 1944. These four supplementary pages are examples of the information, regarding the aircraft of Japan, that was distributed to Air Force units down to the squadron level. This loose leaf book type data was retained for the use of the pilots, aircrewmen, and others by the Intelligence Officers of each unit. When the war was over, I "inherited" the squadron file, of which these "Irving" pages are a small part—this material was no longer of military value. I do think these particular four pages will enhance one of the purposes of this book, namely to let the reader see something "new."

"Irving" was the name given to this twin engine plane by the Allied Forces. Built by Nakajima as the J1N, it was later called Gekko (Moonlight) by the Japanese. The number of all models manufactured amounted to a few less than five hundred planes. Incidentally, the name Gekko was not used until this plane evolved into a night-fighter. I have often wondered if the Japanese had a previous name for this aircraft.

The concept of "Irving" came during an era of military aircraft design in the late thirties that called for multi-seat twin-engined fighter craft. Most air forces of the world subscribed to the theory that a twin-engine fighter plane, with a crew of two or three aboard, could be designed and developed for deep penetration into enemy territory—and still be able to successfully cope with opposing interceptors and fighters in speed, maneuverability, and firepower. History has shown that this idea bore very little fruit. And so it was, also, with the Japanese Navy Air Force in the case of the Nakajima J1N1 "Irving" as a long range fighter. In the very first models there was an unusual rear gun position that consisted of a pair of two-gun remotely controlled turrets, operated by hydraulic power. This heavy arrangement was soon to prove unsatisfactory and was used only with prototype craft.

By the end of 1941, the J1N1 had proved a disappointment in its service trials and thus was ended the high hopes for this plane to be a long-range escort fighter or a penetration fighter. The next step was to rework the plane for duty as a high speed reconnaissance plane and it was in this form that the J1N was first produced in numbers, and put into general service. It was during the Solomons campaign that this twin engine plane was first spotted by the American forces. It was wrongly considered to be a fighter plane and was soon dubbed "Irving."

Any time that one reads about "Irving," there is always recounted the story of its first usage as a night-fighter. This event took place above the great Japanese base at Rabaul on New Britain. The Aussie and American night intruders were taking their toll around the harbor and airfields there, and one of the Japanese

Variations on a Plane by Nakajima: "Irving"

Above is a double-take of the same "Irving," standing alongside a "Frances" twin-engine bomber. One prop has been removed and the rudder has been bashed in. This plane was painted a shade of green unlike any other plane at Atsugi. Look at the shade of green on the seal on the front of a dollar bill—that's as close as you'll get to this plane's unique color. Remarkably, this neat and efficient-looking combat aircraft had the offensive firepower of only one 20mm cannon that was obliquely mounted, firing forward above the mid-fuselage area.

countermeasures was the conversion of a couple of "Irvings," based there, into night-fighters. Unlike most forward firing fixed-gun mounts, two pairs of 20mm cannon were obliquely-installed, two guns being set to fire forward above, and two below, the longitudinal axis of the plane at a 30 degree angle. The rear cockpit area was utilized for this rather peculiar arrangement. As the story goes, on a moonlit night in May of 1943, two raiding American four-engine bombers were shot down in flames by these field-modified airplanes. These early successes prompted the modification in production of "Irving" from that of a high speed reconnaissance plane into that of a bomber interceptor incorporating this unique fixed oblique gun arrangement—with this the "Irving" moved into another phase of its existence.

Chasing down B-24s and intercepting B-29s were two different challenges—and thus another cause for "Irving" that would have only very limited success. "Irving's" struggle continued even up to its occasional sortie as a suicide plane. Again with its use in this regard, its successes may not have been too great—most "Irvings" that I saw lacked gear for bomb-hauling and so their use in body crashing attacks would have been potentially less effective against ships.

All of my photos of "Irving" were taken at Atsugi Naval Air Station in September and October of 1945. There were a good three dozen "Irvings" at that field when the Americans occupied that base and I was able to get a good look at all of them. While "Irving" was manufactured for at least three basic uses during its life, I don't know if I ever saw another type of plane during the war years that had so many sub-variations on so many models. It was almost as if no two planes were just alike—at Atsugi it sure seemed that this was so.

Here are some very close looks at "Irving" that could be of special interest to the model maker and the aviation historian. Very apparent are the fuselage details showing the basic change in model design from that of a three-seat plan, used primarily for high-speed reconnaissance work, into that of a two-seat bomber interceptor.

These photos also reveal some variations within a given model. The turrets are not the same, and there is a noticeable difference about the fuselage area to the rear of the turrets.

Of the many planes at Atsugi, there were only two with a natural finish, and here is one of them. We who saw this plan "in person" admired the quality of the metal work that is quite apparent in this picture.

The next page shows the lines of the last model type "Irving" that was manufactured by Nakajima. Built as a two-seat interceptor, the fuselage had a straight back from the cockpit area to the tail. Some of these later models had radar aboard.

Note the two pairs of obliquely-mounted cannons—one pair angled up and the other down. It is also interesting to note the metallic "windows" in front of the upper guns. I think that this arrangement at the rear of the cockpit had a dual purpose. It would shield the crew from the blinding flash of the firing guns at night and would remove the risk of glass being cracked or shattered by the 20mm cannon's muzzle blast.

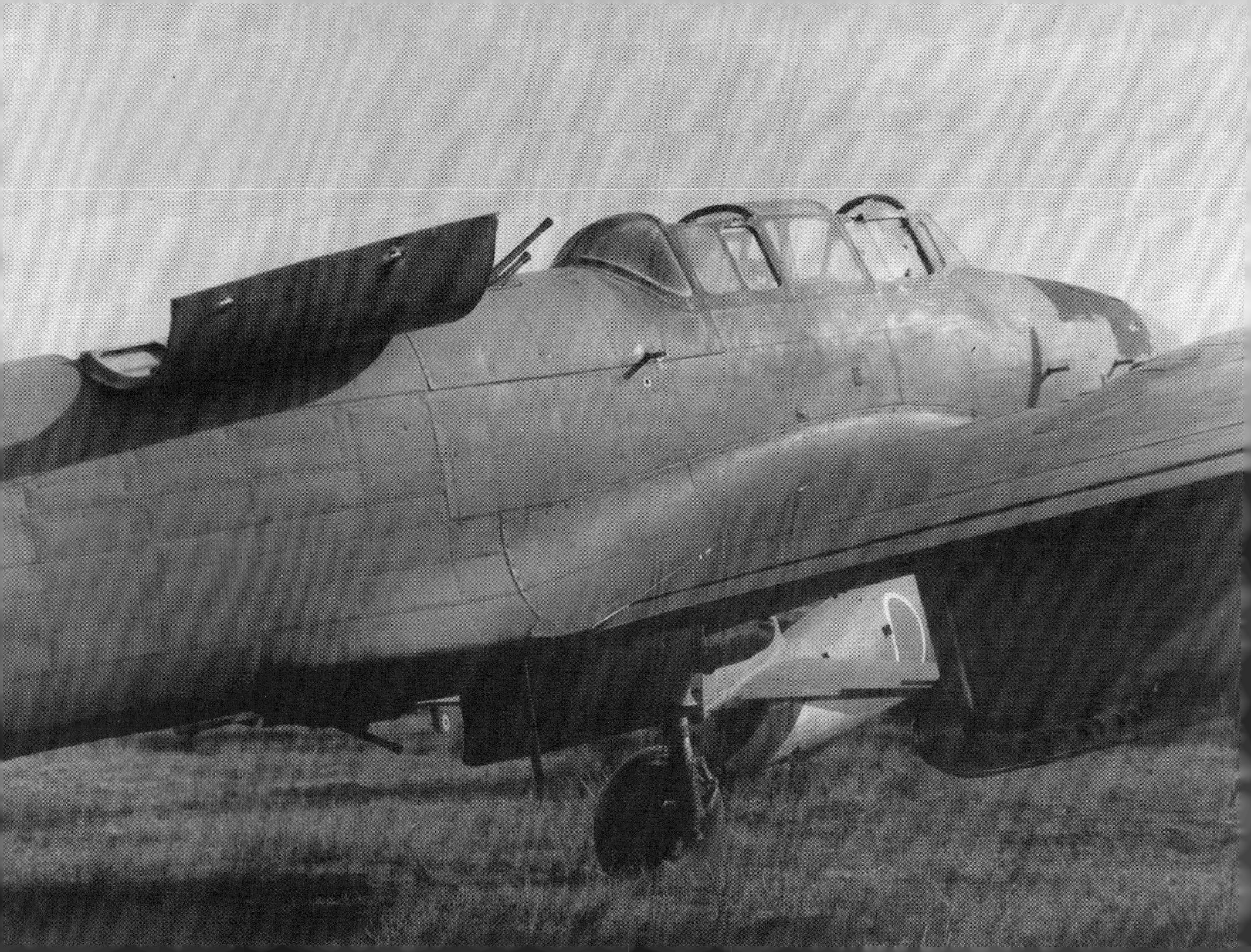

Variations on a Plane by Nakajima: "Irving"

My camera's eye captured a few more looks at "Irving." In the upper photo of this page can be seen five of these planes that have been pushed aside along with some "Jacks" and "Zekes," at one of Atsugi's corners. Several modifications may be seen, including a late model that mounts three 20mm cannons topside aimed to fire obliquely forward. That particular craft is seen just above the cockpit of the plane in the foreground. The "Irving" up front sports a slab of steel behind the pilot's seat, a "luxury" lacking in far too many Japanese aircraft. In the other photo on this page is a full side view of a "recce" type that had been converted to interceptor duty in the field by the mounting of a single 20mm cannon obliquely aimed.

Below, on the next page, is a picture of something I'll wager you have never seen before—it is a really close look at the twin 20mm fixed cannon mount of the "Irving." I straddled the rear fuselage, opened the hatch, and took the shots you see here. This particular plane did not carry the lower gun position. In fact, the ventral twin 20mm cannon assembly was used in only a few of the many "Irvings" that I saw at Atsugi Naval Air Station. There are some more pictures here for you to inspect.

I think that there is an interesting side light on the name given to this Nakajima type aircraft. It had been the policy in code-naming Japanese planes (by the Allies), to make use of male names for fighters and female names for bombers and reconnaissance types. "Irving," when first spotted, was wrongly thought to be a fighter craft, but at that time, it was actually a reconnaissance plane. An "Irving" by any other name may well have been.

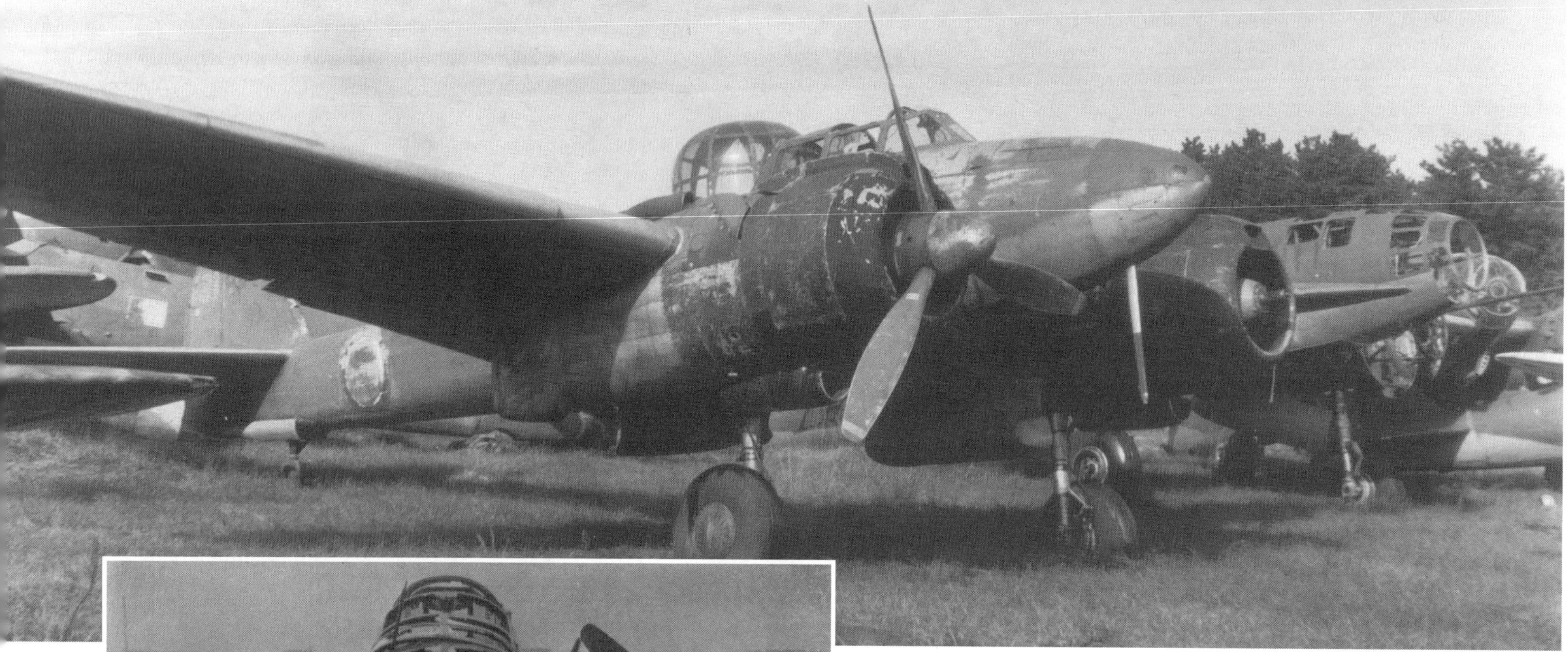

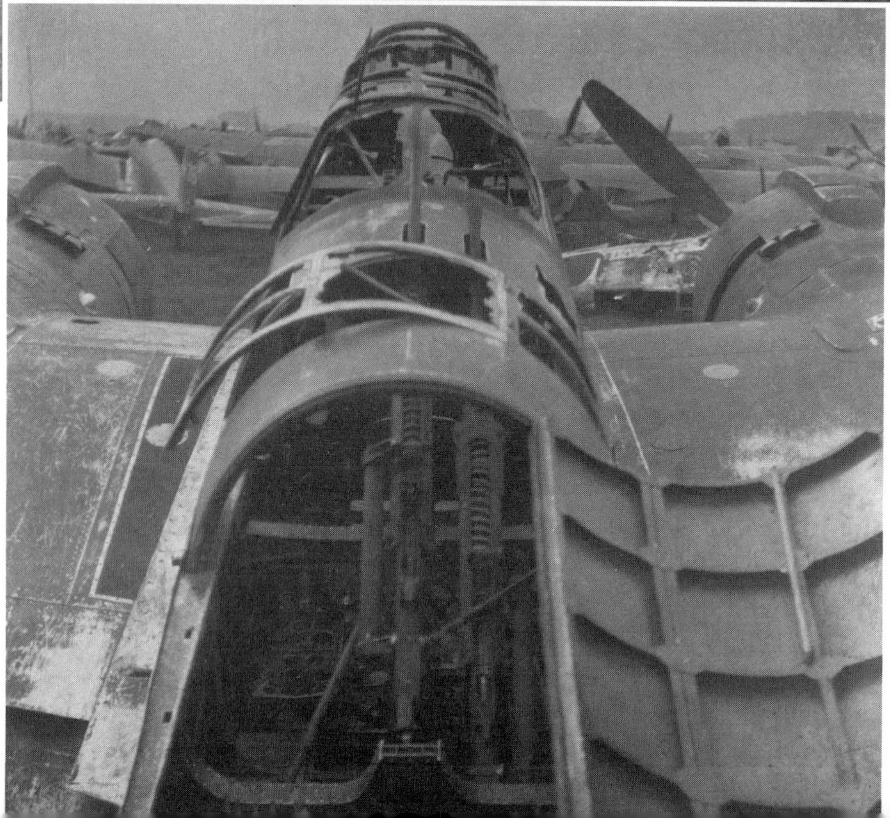

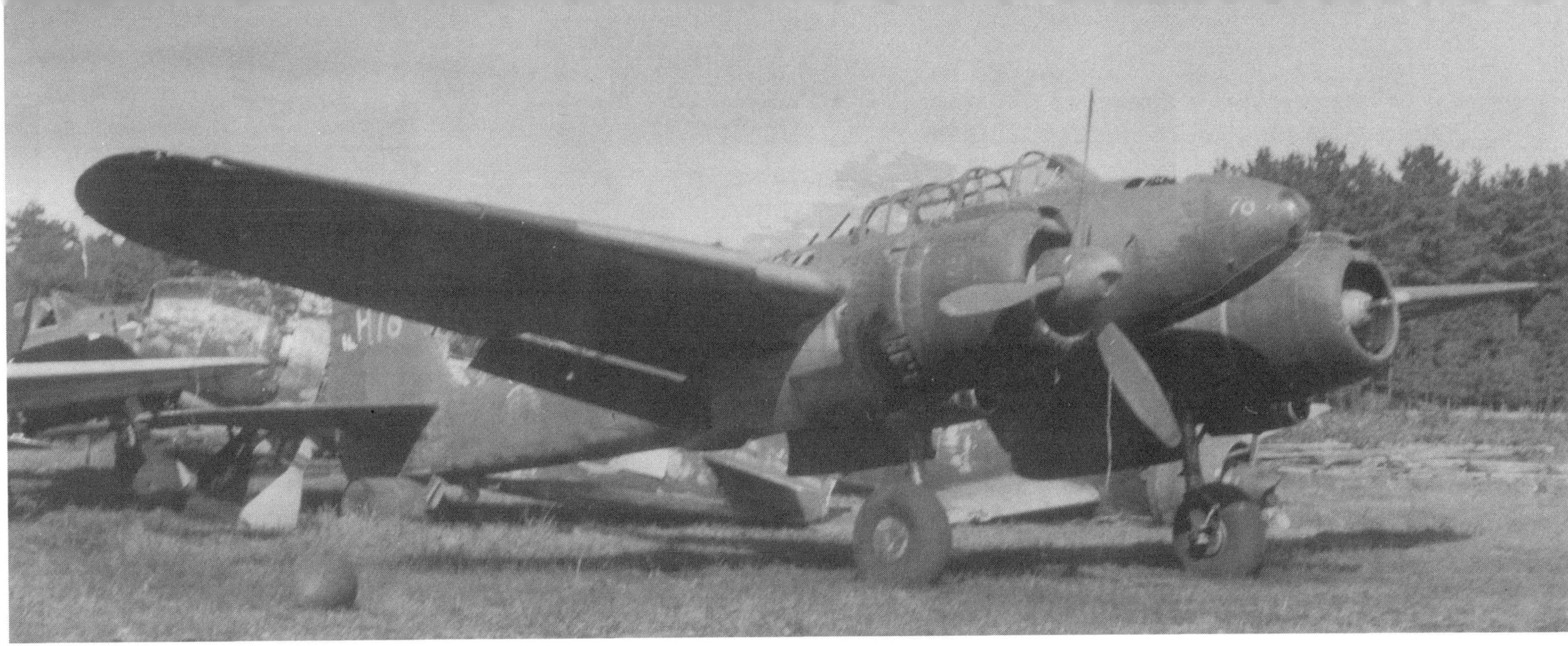

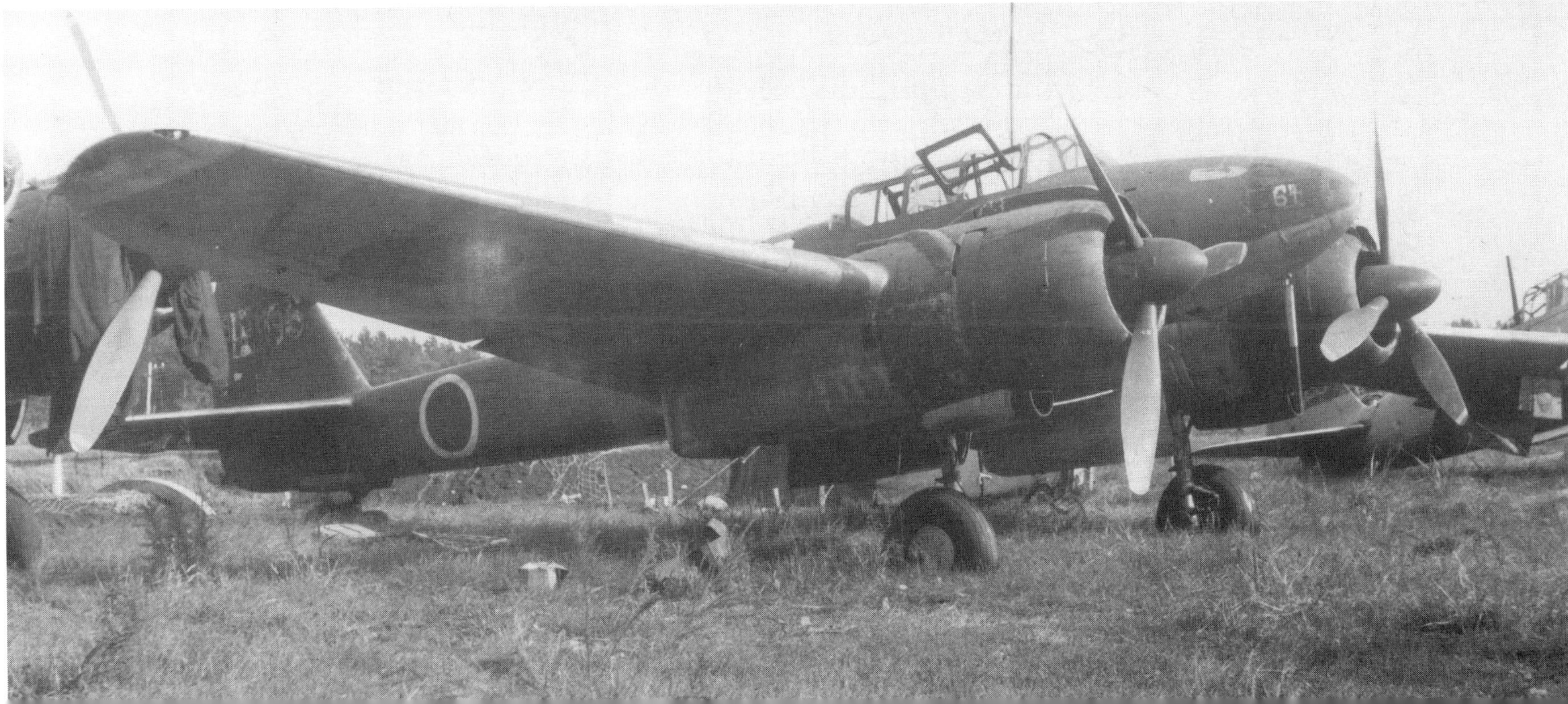

Variations on a Plane by Nakajima: "Irving"

IRVING 11 — RANGE · SPEED · CLIMB

KEY	CONDITION	WEIGHT (lb.)	FUEL LOAD (lb.)	BOMBS—CARGO (lb.)
———	NIGHT FIGHTER with Radar	16600	2886	None
– – –	NIGHT FIGHTER w/o Radar	16400	2886	None
———	RECONNAISSANCE	17544	3930	None

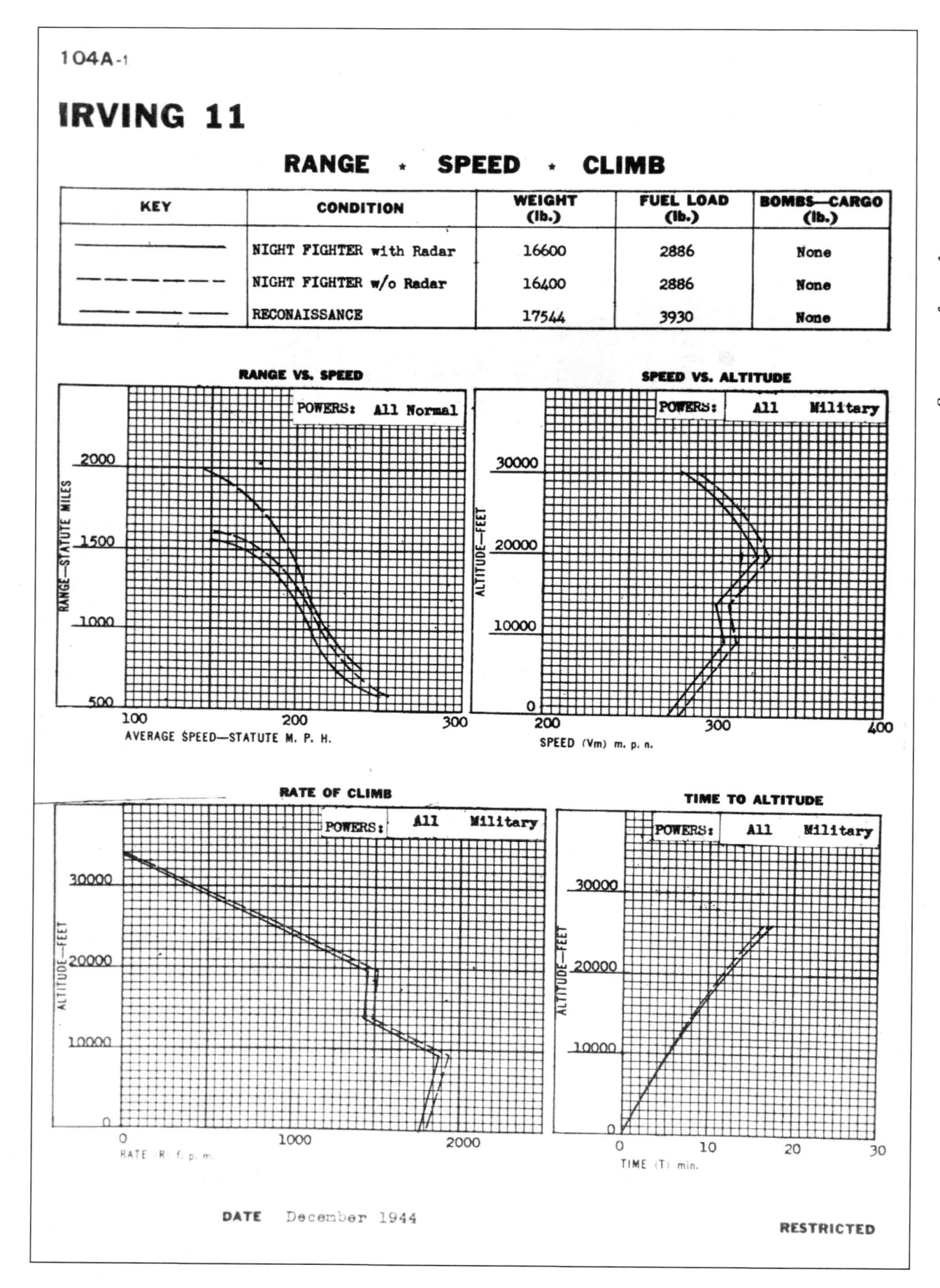

SPEED VS. ALTITUDE — POWERS: All Military

RANGE VS. SPEED — POWERS: All Normal

TIME TO ALTITUDE — POWERS: All Military

RATE OF CLIMB — POWERS: All Military

104A-1   DATE December 1944   RESTRICTED

IRVING 11

104A-2

AIRCRAFT

Duty	Night Fighter
Designation	(GEKKO) Model 11
Description	Low-wing Monoplane
Mfg.	Nakajima
Engines 2	Crew 2
Construction	All metal

ENGINES

H.P.		Altitude
Take-off	1115	S.L.
Normal		
Military	1085	9,350'
War Emerg.	965 / 1180	19,700' / 7,500'

Mfg.	Nakajima
Model	Sakae 21
Type	Radial
Cylinders 14	Cooling Air
Supercharger	2 Speed
Propeller 3 blade C.S. Diam. 10'
Fuel—Take-off 92 Cruising 92

DIMENSIONS

Span 55.7'   Length 39.9'
Height 15'   Wing area 430 sq.ft.

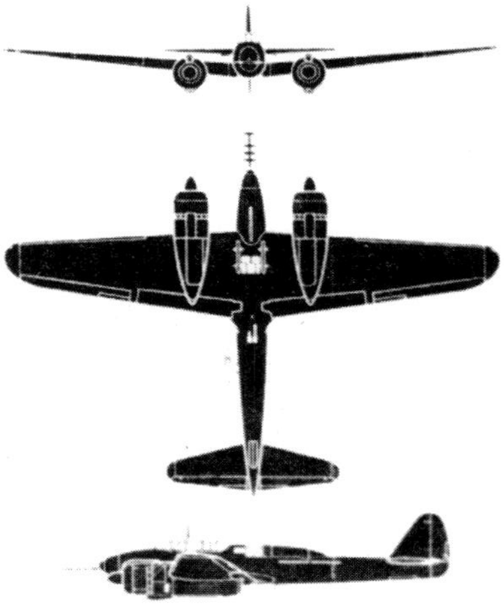

PERFORMANCE AND CHARACTERISTICS

TAKE-OFF

	Load	Feet
T.O. calm	16600	1075
T.O. 25 kt. wind	16600	510
T.O. over 50' obstacle		
Landing over 50' obstacle		

CLIMB—CEILING

@ 16,600 lbs.	Feet	Min.
Rate @ S.L.	1780	1
Rate @ 9,350'	1880	1
Rate @ 19,700 ft.	1460	1
Time to 10,000'		5.5
Time to 20,000'		12.1
Service ceiling	32,740'	

SPEED

@ 16,600 lbs.	Mph.	Knts.	Altitude
Maximum	274	237	@ S.L.
Maximum	333	288	@19,700'
Cruising 75%	188	163	1,500'
Economical			

BOMBS—CARGO

	No.	Size	Total Lbs.
Normal			
Maximum	2	250 kg	1100

WEIGHTS

	Lbs.
Empty	10,700
Gross (Night Fighter)	16,600
Overload (Reconnaissance)	17,544

FUEL

	U.S. gal.	Imp. gal.
Built-in	492	408
Internal (Removable)	174	144
External (drop)	666	552
Maximum		

RANGE AND RADIUS

	Miles stat.	naut.	Speed mph.	Knts.	Alt. feet	Fuel U.S.	Imp.	Bombs lbs.	Cargo lbs.
Maximum range (maximum fuel) @ 75% VM	1985	1725	145	126	1500	666	552	None	None
	1745	1515	181	157	1500	666	552	None	None
Maximum range (normal fuel) @ 75% VM	1560	1354	150	130	1500	492	408	None	None
	1360	1080	188	163	1500	452	408	None	None
Radius ( )									
Radius ( )									

GENERAL DATA

IRVING carries radar and may be used either as a night fighter or for reconnaissance. Except for "Maximum Range with Maximum Fuel", the above figures are based on the night fighter version.

Auxiliary fuel tanks are known to be carried but the 2 x 87 gallon tanks are assumptions.

Internal fuel and lube oil tanks are self-sealing.

RESTRICTED   **DATE** December 1944

Variations on a Plane by Nakajima: "Irving"

IRVING 11

FIELDS OF FIRE

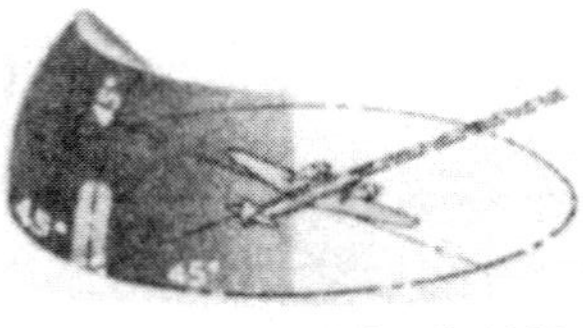

FORWARD GUNS "A", AND "B" AND TOP GUN "C"
rear view from above
Reconnaissance Version

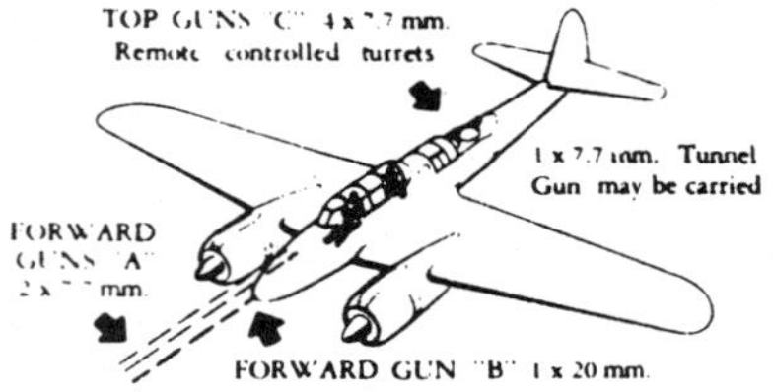

TOP GUNS "C" 4 x 7.7 mm.
Remote controlled turrets

FORWARD GUNS "A"
2 x 20 mm.

FORWARD GUN "B" 1 x 20 mm.

1 x 7.7 mm. Tunnel Gun may be carried

Reconnaissance Version
front view from above

Fuel and Oil tanks and oxygen cylinders are same on both versions

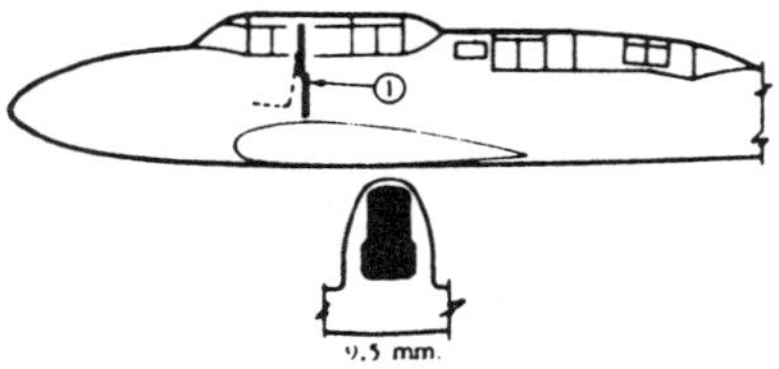

EXHAUST FLAME PATTERNS

REAR VIEW

VULNERABILITY

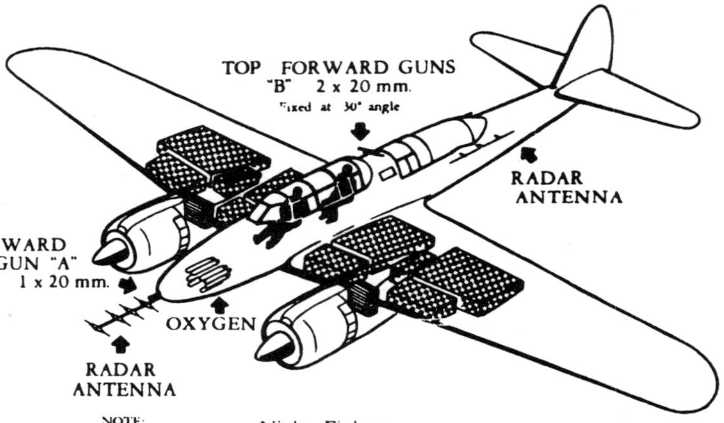

Jettisonable Fuel tanks

BOTTOM FORWARD GUNS "C" 2 x 20 mm.
Fixed at 30° angle

TOP FORWARD GUNS "B" 2 x 20 mm.
Fixed at 30° angle

RADAR ANTENNA

OXYGEN

FORWARD GUN "A" 1 x 20 mm.

RADAR ANTENNA

NOTE: Alternate nose carries landing light in place of gun and radar antenna

Night Fighter Version

LEGEND

| Fuel tanks, unprotected | Oil tanks, unprotected |
| Fuel tanks, protected | Oil tanks, protected |

ARMOR PLATE

9.5 mm.

Viewed from rear

ARMAMENT

	No.	Size	Rds. Gun	Type		No.	Size	Rds. Gun	Type
Forward	1	20 mm	100 (Not always found)	Fixed	Tail				
Top	2	20 mm	100	Fixed	Wing				
Side									
Bottom	1	20 mm	100	Fixed					

TACTICAL DATA

The top and bottom 20 mm guns are mounted to face forward at a fixed angle of 30° from the longitudinal axis of the fuselage.
Armor plate is installed to protect the pilot's back and head.
Armament has varied considerably in recce versions.

DATE December 1944

RESTRICTED

104A-3

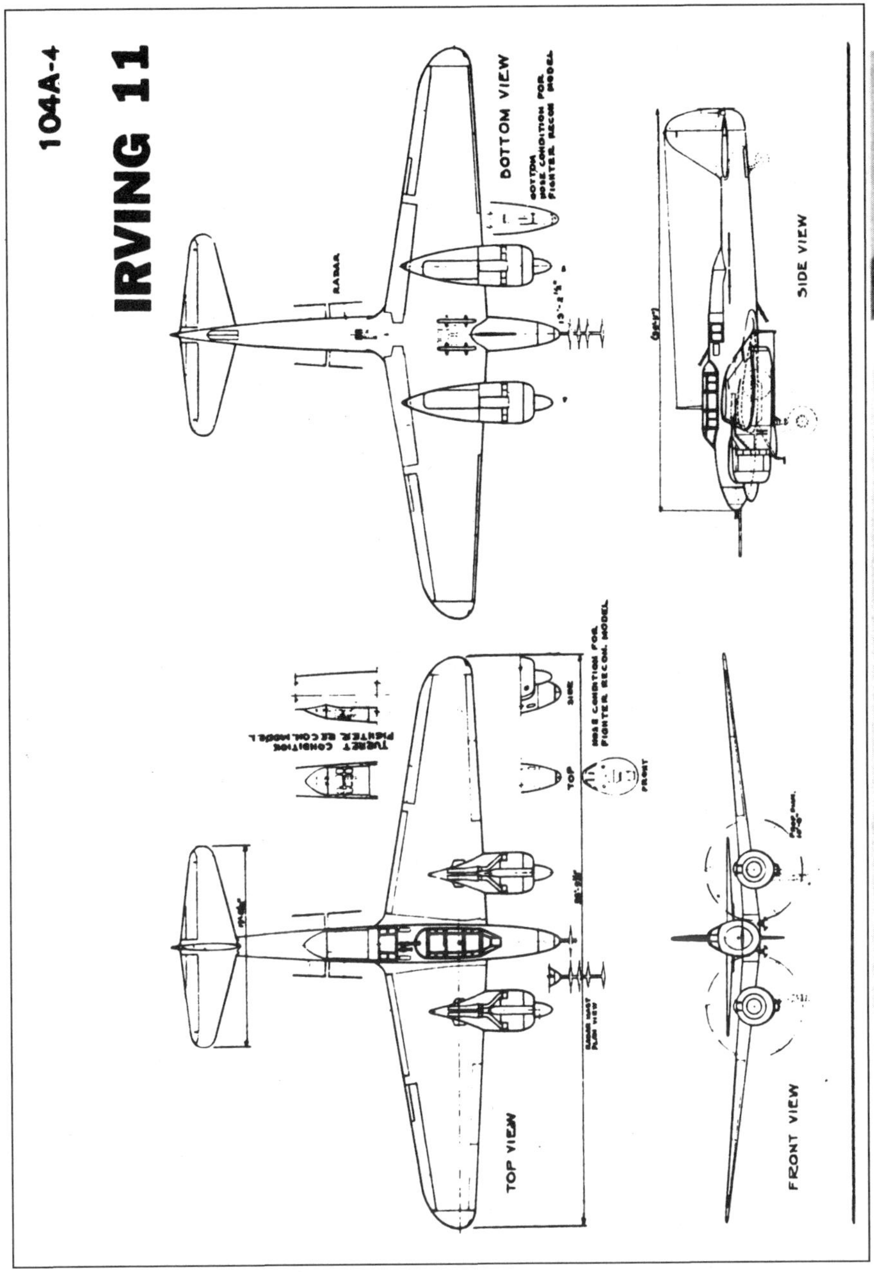

Variations on a Plane by Nakajima: "Irving" 81

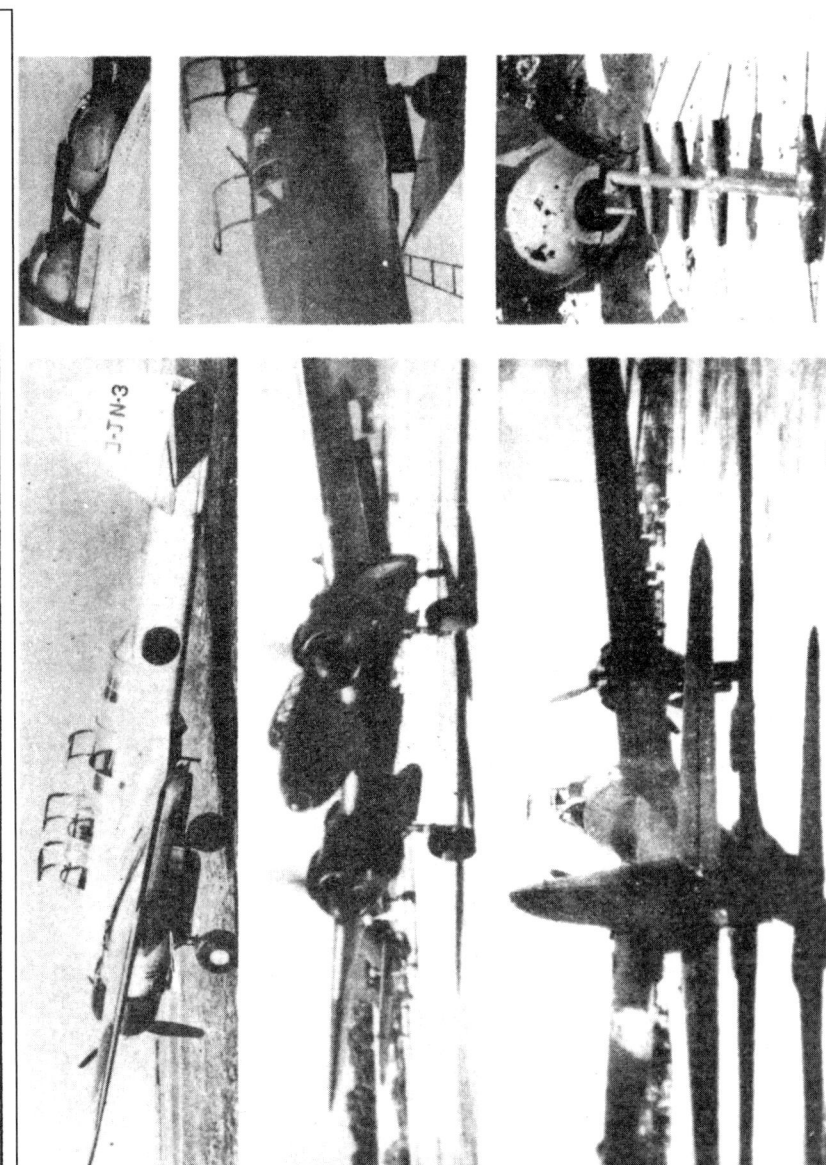

In a Class All by Herself: "Myrt"

Think about it for a minute and then come up with the answer to this question: "Was there such a thing as a long range high speed reconnaissance plane, designed and built as such, used by any navy during World War II?" The answer I come up with is yes, and yet the only plane that I can name is "Myrt" of the Japanese Navy Air Force.

"Myrt" was the name assigned to the Nakajima C6N Saiun (Painted Cloud). This plane first saw action in 1944, and it was designed and equipped for operation from aircraft carriers. However, by the time it was brought into active service, the war had turned into a defensive one for Japan and this "talented" craft's capabilities were severely limited. In fact, its operational career from carriers lasted only a very brief period of time: soon after it came on duty, nearly all of Japan's aircraft carriers were literally knocked out of action or sunk. So "Myrt" became land based and, as such, it was used until the end of the war. There were four or five at Atsugi, and here are pics of two of them.

In looking at "Myrt," take note of the unusual canopy arrangement in the picture on the next page. The front seat could be jacked up higher and a windscreen panel could be locked in an up position. This was done to aid the pilot's vision for carrier take-offs and landings. I was impressed by the small-in-diameter, yet very powerful engine that pulled the plane through the air. The plane was very lightly constructed. In addition, the only armament was a small machine gun position for the rear crewman; there was no armor protection for any of the crew. Obviously, speed was the name of the game for "Myrt."

Although alleged to be as fast as any fighter plane that the U.S. had in combat, radar-directed interception often aided successful attacks to take place against this very speedy plane.

Out in the Pacific, we knew that the Japanese had some crackerjack reconnaissance planes. We knew that radar would pick them up, but more times than enough, the American interceptors could not catch up. Some of us wondered, from late 1944 on, how the Japanese big wheels felt about what was reported back to them—whatever the reports, they certainly couldn't have been too happy about them.

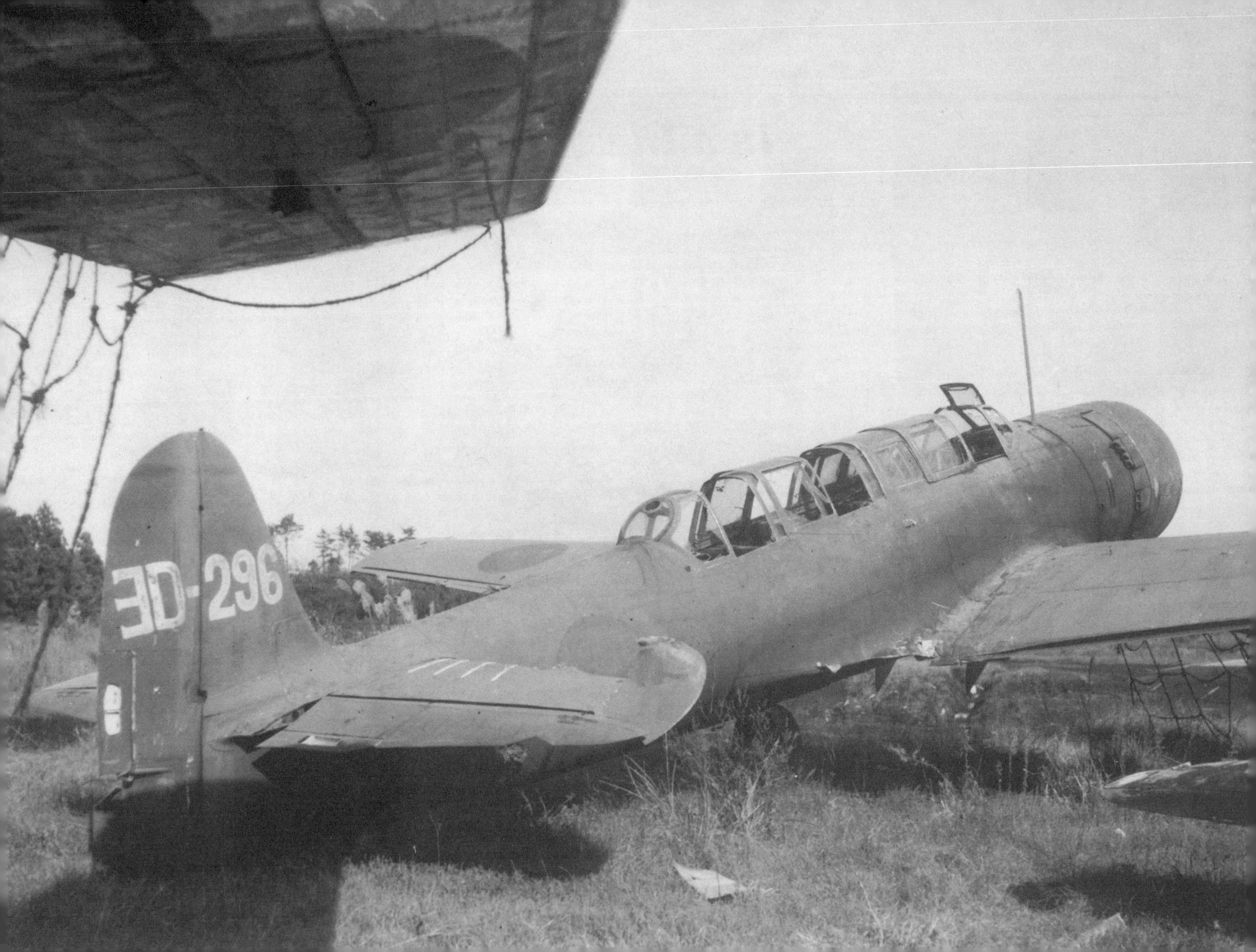
3D-296

"Frances"

Any historian, student of history, or anyone with even a casual interest in the war in the Pacific will recognize the names "Betty" and "Zero" and know something about these two famous warplanes. Some of the aforementioned people will also be able to add the names of the "Val" dive bomber and the "Kate" torpedo bomber, mainly because these planes were used in the Pearl Harbor attack, thereby gaining some fame. Those who have delved a bit deeper into that conflict may recall the names of "Nell" and "Tony" but from then on . . .

Yet, students of air history, as well as military aviation buffs, are aware of the fact that the Japanese Air Forces had many types of planes in combat service that were both good in design and quality, and also substantial in numbers. However, as some new and fine Japanese planes were reaching combat service, the American aircraft they had to face were so excellent in quality and overwhelming in quantity, the worth and potential of these Japanese aircraft was virtually eclipsed. The tempo of war against Japan increased dramatically. For many of those "out there," things were moving so fast by mid 1944 on, there was hardly the time to gain the familiarity of names of enemy aircraft—that is, unless you were mixed in with the air forces, army or navy, around where the action was.

Dropped out of chatter at chow were old names like "Sally," "Lily," "Betty," and "Oscar." Then you heard talk about "Tojo," "Frank," "Jack," and such—the older enemy planes' names were not forgotten, just replaced in thoughts and conversations by the new, exciting, high-performing enemy aircraft.

Among this "new breed" of planes to make its debut during the last twelve-month period of the war was the twin-engine medium bomber called "Frances" by the Allies. "Frances" was designed by the First Naval Air Technical Arsenal at Yokosuka. It was designated the Yokosuka P1Y1 Ginga (Milky Way) Navy Bomber by the Japanese, and the principal builder was Nakajima, who made just under one thousand airframes. Close to a hundred additional airframes, modified mainly for night interception duty, were made by Kawanishi. This night fighter modification was called Kyokko (Aurora) by the Japanese.

These designations, Milky Way and Aurora, tend to make me digress a moment regarding the rather picturesque and colorful names given their military planes. Contemplate some of these translations from the Japanese: Violent Wind, Heavenly Thunder, Flying Swallow, Demon, Falcon, Hurricane, Flying Dragon, Dragon Swallower, Dragon Killer, Violet Lightning, Thunderbolt, Mighty Wind, Heavenly Mountain, Shooting Star, Painted Cloud—there were other names just as striking, yet romantic and ethereal, considering the fact that these planes were actually machines of war.

But back to "Frances," the plane that was made to replace the "Betty" in the service of the Japanese Navy. During its relatively short duty in combat, "Frances" enjoyed a high reputation among the Allies. We Army Air Force people, who had the rare opportunity to examine several of these planes at Atsugi, after the war, were very favorably impressed with what we saw. Yet, no one there would have been willing to trade it for the B-25 or B-26, just to name two standard twin-engine planes used by the Allies.

"Frances" was called upon to perform many varied missions; long range attack bomber, torpedo bomber, high level bomber, night interceptor, night intruder, search plane and even a dive bomber (for which it was especially constructed and aided by retractable air brakes). This plane also joined in on the suicide attack parade of Japanese planes. "Frances" was about to be modified into a carrier of the human bomb but time and the war ran out, aborting that plan.

"Frances" was certainly a very fine plane, beautiful in design, especially speedy, and needing a crew of but three to perform its varied capabilities ("Betty" needed 5 to 8). However good a plane it was, when compared to its contemporary like-types of all the other warring nations, it was lacking in both offensive and defensive gun weaponry in most of the planes produced. I have a few "Frances" pics to show you here—could be you'll see a few things you have never seen before—or even knew about. All were taken at Atsugi in September or October 1945.

Incidentally, when did "Frances" first enter combat duty? One Japanese (translated into English) source mentions that in March of 1945 this plane joined operations for the first time. Didn't I see a few "Franceses" making low passes at Tacloban Airstrip on Leyte in late October and early November of 1944? I think so, but I wouldn't swear to it.

Here we have a close-up at the front end of a "Frances" that bore the stenciled number 943. There's a good bit of detail revealed here, including the installation of the radar antennae, one up front and the other on the side of the fuselage near the tail. Clearly shown is the location of the flexible nose-gun mount. The bomb bay doors are retracted here, while the "Frances" in the left background has its doors closed.

At any rate, although I did not plan on it at first, the dearth of information published on "Frances" led me to feel that these five pages of intelligence data should be included here. While the pictures I took will interest the model maker and air buff, the aviation historian may find these pages of particular note. Observe the date of the publication, and check the combat camera pictures of "Frances," as well as the pic of the remains of the nose section of one of these planes.

Here are two looks at the same plane—in fact when I think of this type plane, the "Frances," of the more than two dozen I saw, it is this particular craft that stands out foremost in my memory. Even when I look at these pictures now, it almost seems that I took them just a few years ago and not decades in the past.

Its color was a little brighter green than most of its companion planes, and the rather poor paint job had weathered too fast, letting much bright aluminum show, giving the plane a strange and almost truculent look. The number 181 on its tail was painted over the former designation of 305. The white bands around the Hinomarus had been greened in.

What looked to me like either a 37mm or 40mm field piece was mounted obliquely behind the cockpit, aimed forward. Let's climb out on the wing and take a closer look at things. Wow! How'd you like to be in that cockpit when that cannon lets loose with a few rounds over your head, especially at night? Going after a B-29 in this plane would certainly make for a

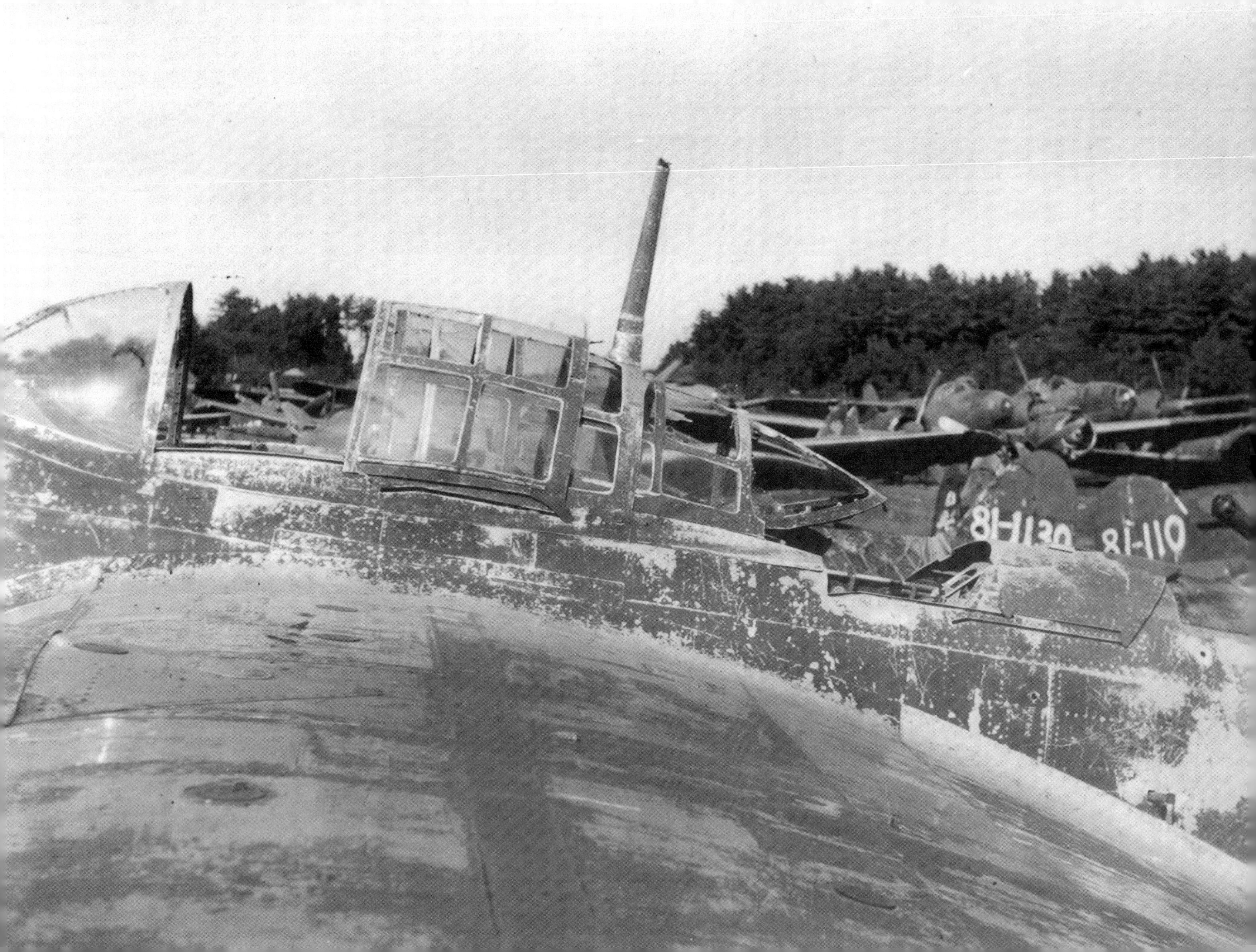
81-130
81-110

night to remember. Anyway, here is a plane for you to remember.

Here are a few more looks at "Frances." Above is a photo of one that, from all appearances to me, was equipped for night search duty. Its color was an earthen green-brown on the upper surfaces and a light gray on the bottom areas. The Hinomarus' white outlines were all hidden by the repainting of their normal red with a rust color that was carried beyond the previous border. Note how flat was the finish of this plane—no lustre at all on this paint job. Also note the simple mount for a light machine gun at the rear of the cockpit. Incidentally, of all the dozens and dozens of planes that I saw equipped for various kinds of night duties, only one was finished in black. That particular craft was a "Lily," and is shown on page XX.

At left is a shot of Lt. Bob Cooper of St. Joseph, Missouri, a P-38 pilot for the 7th Fighter Squadron, 49th Fighter Group. He is checking the controls of a "Frances." Observe the armor shield behind the pilot's seat and speculate awhile on the reasons for this unique adjustable installation. Below that pic is a photo showing the result of a "Frances" being shoved aside by a bulldozer—a broken back. The touch of a 'dozer's blade was, to this formerly ready-to-fly "Frances," the kiss of death.

Here are two more shots of "Frances:" a three-quarter front view of a radar equipped bomber craft, and a full side view of one that was modified for use as a night interceptor having a fixed 20mm cannon obliquely mounted behind the cockpit.

The next five pages display some data originally gathered for dissemination to the U.S. airmen on the "Frances." There should be some interesting "stuff" here to examine.

92 "*Frances*"

FRANCES 11   RANGE · SPEED · CLIMB

303A-1

KEY	CONDITION	WEIGHT (lb.)	FUEL LOAD (lb.)	BOMBS—CARGO (lb.)
——	NORMAL BOMBER	23150	3530	1100
– – –	OVERLOAD TORPEDO	26460	5840	1765
— · —	RECONNAISSANCE (Max. Fuel)	28450	9400	None
——	BOMBER (Max. Fuel)	29180	8420	1765

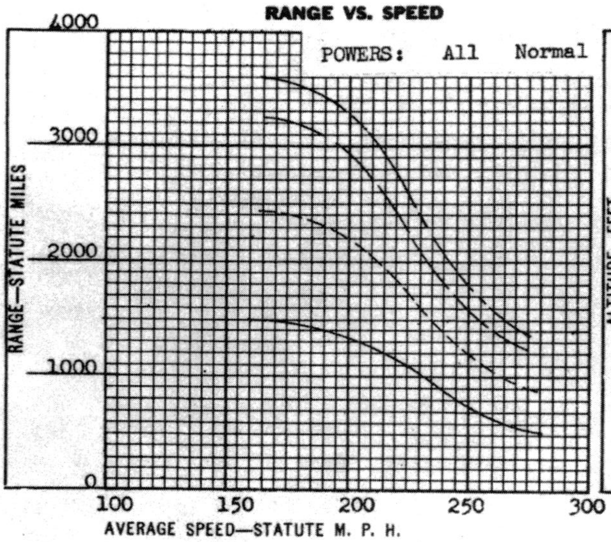

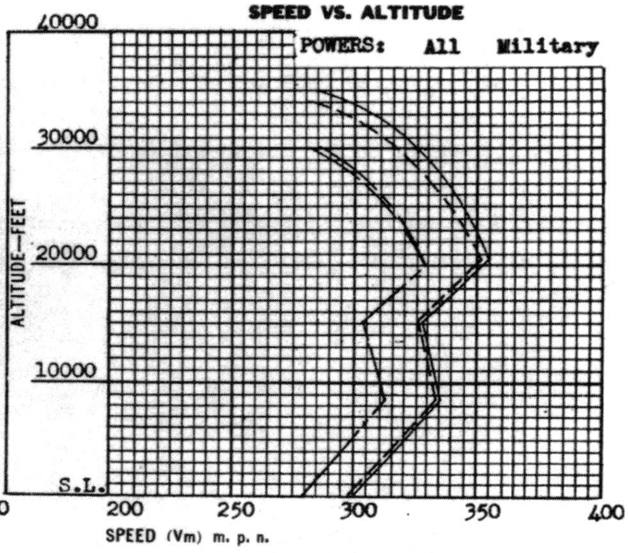

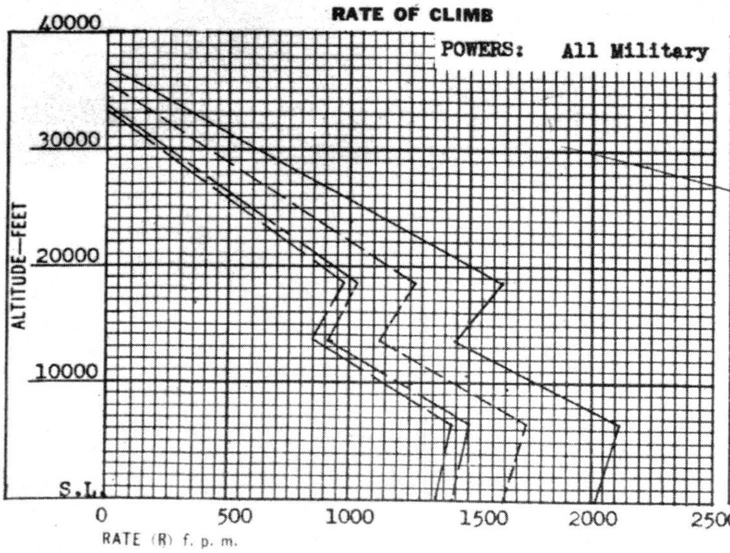

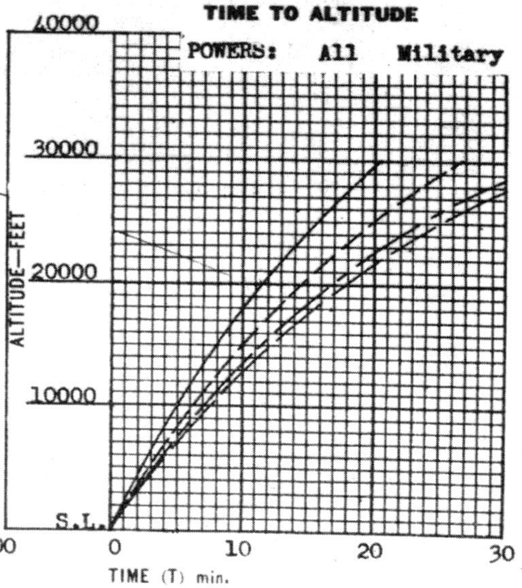

DATE December 1944

RESTRICTED

FRANCES 11

AIRCRAFT

Duty	Medium & Torpedo Bomber
Designation	GINKA, Model 11
Description	Mid-Wing Monoplane
Mfg.	Nakajima
Engines	2 Crew 3
Construction	All Metal

ENGINES

	H.P.	Altitude
Take-off	1795	S.L.
Normal	1295	9,500'
	1130	19,800'
Military	1625	6,560'
	1420	18,700'
War Emerg.	1840	3,020'

Mfg. Nakajima
Model Homare 11
Type Radial
Cylinders 18   Cooling Air
Supercharger 2 Speed
Propeller 3 Blade Diam. 11.5'
C.S.
Fuel - Take-off 92 Cruising 92 plus methanol

DIMENSIONS

Span 65.6'   Length 49.2'
Height 17.4'   Wing area 592 sq.ft.

PERFORMANCE AND CHARACTERISTICS

TAKE-OFF

	Load	Feet
T.O. calm	23,150	1018
	29,180	1480
T.O. 25 kt. wind	23,150	476
	29,180	700
T.O. over 50' obstacle		
Landing over 50' obstacle		

CLIMB—CEILING

	lbs.	Feet	Min.
@ 23,150		2015	1
Rate @ S.L.			
Rate @ 18,600ft.		1630	1
Time to 10,000			5.0
Time to 20,000			11.3
Service ceiling		35,900'	

SPEED

	Mph.	Knts.	Altitude
@ 23150 lbs.			
Maximum	300	261	@ S.L.
Maximum	355	308	@ 20,600'
Cruising 75%	210	183	1,500'
Economical			

BOMBS—CARGO

	No.	Size	Total lbs
Normal or	1	800 kg	1771
	1	800 kg Torp.	1870
Maximum	2	500 kg	2231

WEIGHTS

	Lbs.
Empty	14,665
Gross	23,150
Overload	29,180

FUEL

	U.S. gal.	Imp. gal.
Built-in	998	830
Internal (Removable)	276	229
External (drop)	292	242
Maximum	1566	1301

RANGE AND CARGO

	Miles stat.	naut.	Speed mph.	Knts.	Alt. feet	Fuel gal. U.S.	Imp.	Bombs lbs.	Cargo lbs.
Maximum range At (maximum fuel) 75% V max.	3600	3126	165	143	1500	1566	1301	None	None
	3150	2735	207	180	1500	1566	1301	None	None
Maximum range At (95% fuel) 75% V max.	2425	2106	164	142	1500	998	830	1765	None
	2075	1802	209	181	1500	998	830	1765	None
Radius ( )									
Radius ( )									

GENERAL DATA

FRANCES is expected to be used primarily as a torpedo bomber and secondarily for level and dive bombing. A night fighter version with KASEI 25 engines is expected to have increased fire power. Use of radar in the night fighter version is considered probable. (See sheet 303B)

DATE December 1944

94 "Frances"

FRANCES 11 (Torpedo bomber version)

EXHAUST FLAME PATTERNS

REAR VIEW

ARMOR PLATE

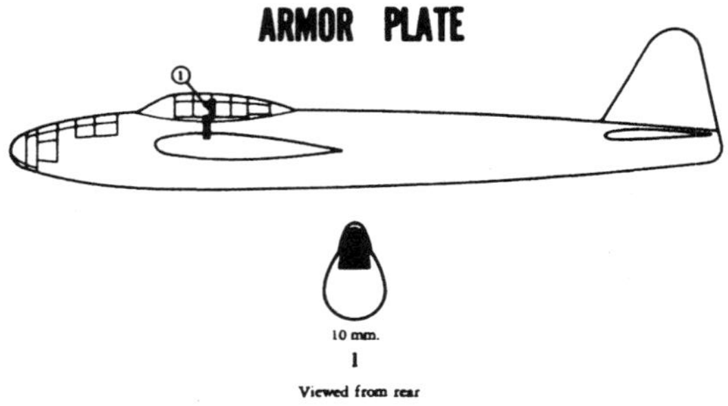

10 mm.

Viewed from rear

VULNERABILITY

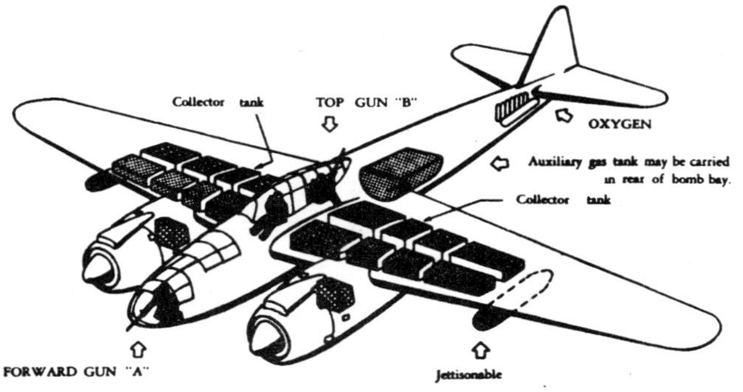

OXYGEN
Auxiliary gas tank may be carried in rear of bomb bay.
Collector tank
TOP GUN "B"
Jettisonable
Collector tank
FORWARD GUN "A"

Two jettisonable gas tanks may be carried in bomb bay in place of bomb load.

LEGEND

| Fuel tanks, protected | Oil tanks, protected |
| Fuel tanks, unprotected | Oil tanks, unprotected |

FIELDS OF FIRE

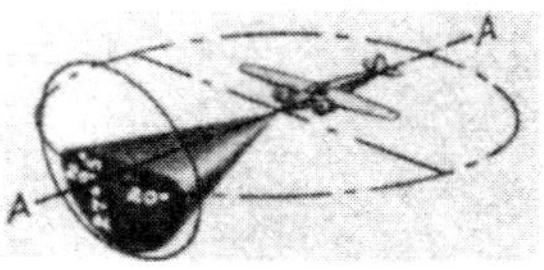

FORWARD GUN "A" 1 x 20 mm.
¾-front view from above
Turret can be rotated mechanically thru 360° about axis "A"-"A"

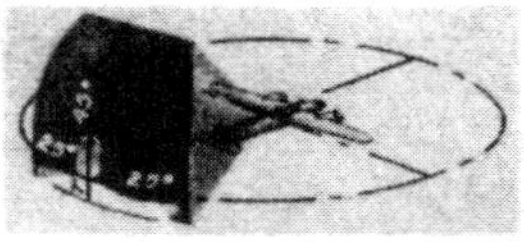

TOP GUN "B" 1 x 20 mm.
¾-rear view from above

FIRE FREE FIELDS

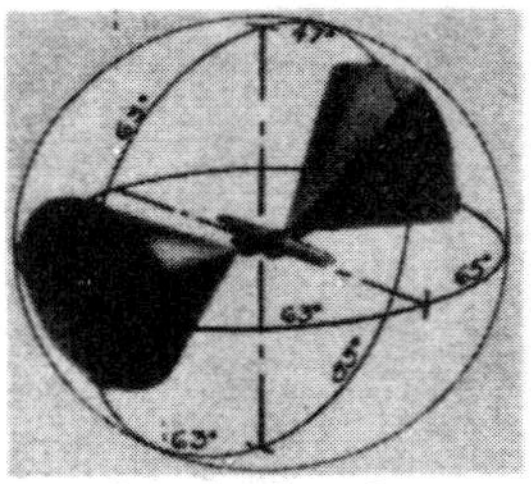

¾-front view from above
FORWARD GUN shows full rotation coverage.

ARMAMENT

	No.	Size	Rds. Gun	Type		No.	Size	Rds. Gun	Type
Forward	1	20 mm	135	Flexible	Tail				
Top					Wing				
Rear									
Cockpit	1	20 mm	225	Flexible					
Side									
Bottom									

TACTICAL DATA

Of the eight fixed fuel tanks in each wing, four are leak proofed. The three additional fuselage tanks and the two underwing tanks are of conventional construction (non-leak proof).

Armor plate is provided for the pilot's seat and head. There are indications that some armor protection is provided the fuel tanks.

DATE December 1944

RESTRICTED

"Frances" 95

FRANCES 11
303A-4

DATE December 1944

RESTRICTED

"Frances"

FRANCES 12 (?) 106A-2

AIRCRAFT

Duty	Night Fighter
Designation	(HAKKŌ) Model 12
Description	Mid-wing Monoplane
Mfg.	Nakajima
Engines	2 Crew 3
Construction	All Metal

ENGINES

	H.P.	Altitude
Take-off	1885	S.L.
Normal		
Military	1655	6,900'
	1520	18,050'
War Emerg.	1735	16,800'

Mfg. Mitsubishi
Model KASEI 25
Type Radial
Cylinders 14   Cooling Air
Supercharger 2 Speed
Propeller 4 Blade Diam. 11.2' C.S.
Fuel - Take-off 92 Cruising 92 plus methanol

DIMENSIONS

Span 65.6'   Length 49.2'
Height 17.4' Wing area 592 sq.ft.

PERFORMANCE AND CHARACTERISTICS

TAKE-OFF

	Load	Feet
T.O. calm	23,940	887
T.O. 25 kt. wind	23,940	422
T.O. over 50' obstacle		
Landing over 50' obstacle		

CLIMB — CEILING

		lbs.	Feet	Min.
@ 23,940	Rate @ S.L.		1910	1
	Rate @ 6900 ft.		2065	1
	Time to 10,000'			5.1
	Time to 20,000'			11.2
	Service ceiling		35,600'	

SPEED

	Mph.	Knts.	Altitude
@ 23,940 lbs.			
Maximum	293	254	@ S.L.
Maximum	354	307	@ 20,050'
Cruising 75%	207	180	1,500'
Economical			

BOMBS — CARGO

	No.	Size	Total Lbs
Normal	None		
Maximum	None		

WEIGHTS

	Lbs.
Empty	17950
Gross	23940
Overload	25835

FUEL

	U.S. gal.	Imp. gal.
Built-in	998	828
Internal (Removable)		
External (drop)	276	229
Maximum	*1274	1057

RANGE AND RADIUS

	Miles		Speed		Alt.	Fuel gal.		Bombs	Cargo
	stat.	naut.	mph.	Knts.	feet	U.S.	Imp.	lbs.	lbs.
Maximum range At 75% Vmax. (maximum fuel)	2925	2540	159	137	1500	1274	1057	None	None
	2465	2140	205	178	1500	1274	1057	None	None
Maximum range At 75% Vmax. (normal fuel)	2385	2071	159	137	1500	998	828	None	None
	1980	1464	207	180	1500	998	828	None	None
Radius ( )									
Radius ( )									

GENERAL DATA

Except for engines and armament no substantial difference is noted between the bomber and night fighter versions of FRANCES. Radar is undoubtedly carried in the night fighter.

*The fuselage tank of 306 gallons carried in FRANCES 11 has been eliminated in the calculations for FRANCES 12 (?) to allow room for additional night fighter equipment.

Silhouette shown is FRANCES 11.

RESTRICTED   DATE December 1944

"Frank": The Fastest Fighter in Service with Japan's Air Forces

The three photographs that follow show a Nakajima Ki-84 taken at Chofu Army Air Base, in the Tokyo area, in September of 1945. It was one of a couple of dozen found at that base after the surrender. In fact, I understand that there were hundreds of this type plane based throughout many airfields of Japan at war's end. I feel sure that this was so because this was the standard Army fighter plane after the fall of 1944 through 1945. This plane was called the Hayte (Gale or Hurricane) by the Japanese and was dubbed "Frank" when it was finally identified by the Americans in the Philippines at the end of '44.

During the war the most famous Japanese aircraft was the "Zero." However, the "Frank" became the most discussed and most written about Japanese warplane after it was all over. In early 1945 it was determined, by extensive Army Air Force tests of warbirds left behind by withdrawing Japanese forces on Luzon, that "Frank" was the fastest plane in their air arsenal. In addition, its maneuverability was considered outstanding. Naturally this information was made known

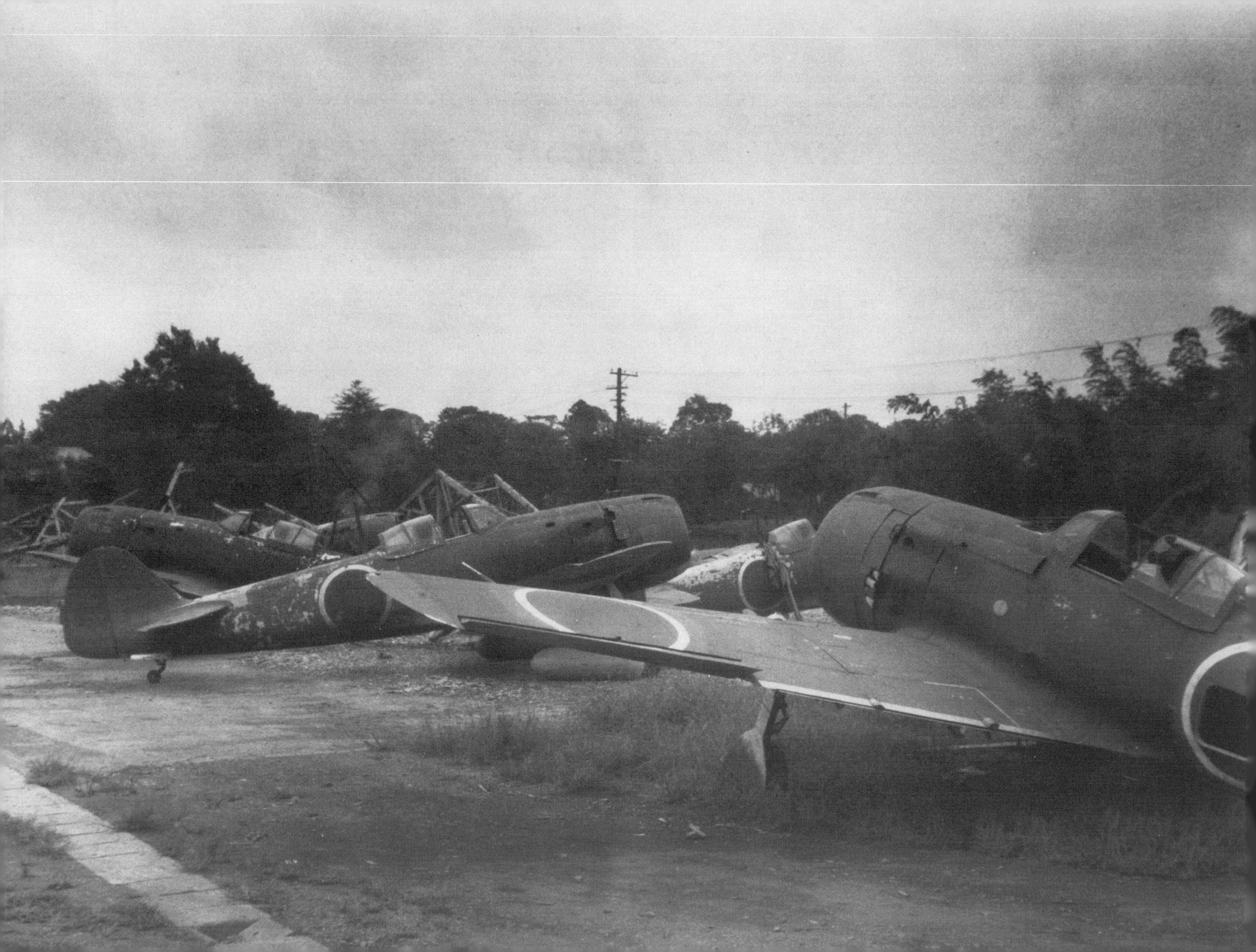

to the U.S. military forces in the Pacific and caused a good bit of talk, especially among the American fighter pilots. Thus began the legend of the "Frank."

After the war, when the lid was off restricted data, these Clark Field (on Luzon) tests became broadly known. Competitive tests, pitting "Frank" against various Allied craft, continued for a short period of time. Comparisons are recounted of the matching of "Frank" with the latest P-51s and P-47s—and just how superb "Frank" had proven to be. It was rated a match for the renowned P-51 "Mustang," and more than one for the latest P-47 "'Thunderbolt," both in speed and maneuverability.

On the intelligence page after the photos of "Frank," take note of the sparsity of information that was gathered at that time. The date on this document was December, 1944 and the very little data exhibited was even qualified as "provisional"—and this plane was very much involved in the campaign for Leyte.

This, I think, brings up an interesting point that is not meant to belittle "Frank," but to point out the greatness of the P-38 "Lightning." After the great naval battles for Leyte Gulf, with most of the Japanese fleet wrecked or driven back, the bulk of the U.S. Navy in the area was withdrawn for repairs and replenishment. Right after that momentous sea-air battle, P-38s of the 49th Fighter Group arrived at their new base on Tacloban, Leyte, on October 27, 1944, to be exact. Their initial task was to defend the new beachhead from the freewheeling Japanese air assaults that were then taking place. For a period of time it was that crack fighter group against any and all planes that the Japanese were able to muster against the new arrived American forces. The truly spectacular success of the P-38s at Leyte and Mindoro is another story that will be told at length some day, but there is a point to make here. At that time I would hear some of the 49th pilots describe some of their victories over planes at and around Leyte (besides the easily identified aircraft) as "an Oscar-like fighter," a plane that was "a big Oscar," or "an Oscar-plus plane," and even "a speedy gosh-knows." They were mixing it up with the "Frank" without even knowing it at the time.

These aggressive pilots with their beloved P-38's were absolutely undaunted by the appearances of any enemy aircraft regardless of number or type—identifiable or not.

Sure, the "Frank" was a great fighter plane, but I know of one that was a little bit better.

"Frank": The Fastest Fighter in Service with Japan's Air Forces

FRANK 1

AIRCRAFT

Duty	Fighter
Designation	Ki 84
Description	Low-wing Monoplane
Mfg.	Nakajima
Engines	1 Crew 1
Construction	All Metal

ENGINES

	H.P.	Altitude
Take-off	1970	S.L.
Normal	1150	8,000'
	1000	22,000'
Military	1875	5,900'
	1675	19,600'
War Emerg.	2050	2,500'

Mfg. Nakajima
Model Ha 45   Model 21
Type Radial
Cylinders 18   Cooling Air
Supercharger 2 Speed
Propeller 4 Blade Diam. 10'
        C.S. Electric
Fuel - Take-off 92 Cruising 92
        (plus methanol)

DIMENSIONS

Span 37.1'   Length 32.3'
Height 11.2'   Wing area 266 sq.ft.

PERFORMANCE AND CHARACTERISTICS

TAKE-OFF

	Load	Feet
T.O. calm	7940	686
T.O. 25 kt. wind	9194	1019
T.O. over 50' obstacle		
Landing over 50' obstacle		

CLIMB—CEILING

	lbs.	Feet	Min.
@	7940		
Rate @ S.L.		3780	1
Rate @ 21,000 ft.		3290	1
Time to 10,000			2.7
Time to 20,000			5.8
Time to 30,000			9.8
Service ceiling		39,000'	

SPEED

@ 7940 lbs.	Mph.	Knts.	Altitude
Maximum	348	302	@ S.L.
Maximum	422	367	@ 21,000'
	396	344	@ 30,000'
Cruising 75%	219	190	1,500'
Economical			

BOMBS—CARGO

	No.	Size	Total Lbs.
Normal	None		
Maximum	2	30 kg	132

WEIGHTS

	Lbs.
Empty	
Gross	7940
Overload	9194

FUEL

	U.S. gal.	Imp. gal.
Built-in		
Internal (Removable)	185	154
External (drop)	174	144
Maximum	359	298

RANGE AND RADIUS

	Miles stat.	naut.	Speed Mph.	Knts.	Alt. feet	Fuel U.S.	gal. Imp.	Bombs lbs.	Cargo lbs.
Maximum range (maximum fuel)	1795	1560	156	135	1500	359	298	None	None
At 75% Vmax.	1535	1330	195	169	1500	359	298	None	None
Maximum range (normal fuel)	1125	977	176	153	1500	185	154	None	None
At 75% Vmax.	930	807	219	190	1500	185	154	None	None
Radius ( )									
Radius ( )									

GENERAL DATA

Normal fighter weight, fuel capacity, dimensions, area military and take-off power are all documentary values.
Drag analysis is based on areas and dimensions and the assumption that the plane will have lines similar to OSCAR since there is no evidence as to the physical appearance of the plane. Dimensions given are similar to those of OSCAR and it is quite certain this plane is of Nakajima design.
Performance figures should be taken as estimates but they do give an indication of the expected performance of new Japanese fighters.

RESTRICTED   Provisional Data   DATE December 1944

The Nakajima Ki-87: "Big Boy"

The plane seen in this segment of the book is actually a one and only. We see an experimental high altitude interceptor fighter that was built by Nakajima for the Japanese Army Air Forces and designated Ki-87. Although most of Japan's later aircraft of the war had nicknames, I have neither heard nor seen in print one of those very colorful Japanese nicknames assigned to this one. Also this is one of several different Japanese experimental planes that the Allies were unaware of during the war, and thus there was no so-called Allied code name tacked on it.

Some of us of the 49th Fighter Group made a couple of virtual pilgrimages to inspect this aircraft. I say pilgrimages because of the considerable distance from Atsugi to where the Ki-87 was, the difficulty of borrowing a jeep or other transport, the rough roads to travel, the rather limited supply of gasoline, the ease of getting lost as we had no road maps, and the fact that if you did get lost, nobody around the countryside could speak English. Those first days of the occupation were not ones of plenty and convenience!

The Nakajima Ki-87: "Big Boy"

This airplane was found at Chofu Army Air Base. The U.S. authorities had it, a Nakajima Ki-115 Tsurugi and also a Kawasaki Ki-100 "Radial Tony" set aside from the crop of fighters there for the purpose of later evaluation. The Ki-87 was literally tagged (in the pics note the tag tied to the prop) for preservation, and was scheduled to be dismantled and shipped back to the United States for analysis by the U.S. Army Air Forces. It was at that time (September and October 1945) under constant guard. This was done to protect this unique plane from any kind of damage, intentional or otherwise—I think mainly to protect it from the ravages of souveniring.

We who saw this plane "in person" know that there was nothing like it anywhere, and there was no manual to give us a code name for it. Obviously, it was a fighter aircraft designed for high altitude work and we felt it should have some kind of a name, as had been the custom of the times. We therefore, although certainly unofficially, gave it the name of "Big Boy," a name that seemed very appropriate. It was surely the largest single-engine fighter plane any of us had ever seen or even heard of. Dimensionally, it even exceeded the U.S. Army's huge P-47 "Thunderbolt," which at that time was thought to be the paragon of bigness for a single-engine fighter.

After the war was over, we Americans found out that the Japanese had begun to manufacture and test both jet and rocket types of combat planes. These particular types of craft followed very closely the German precedent almost to the point of sameness. Only a handful of each was made in the last month or so of the war and were never reported to have reached combat status. The Nakajima Ki-87, however, stuck very definitely to the Japanese school of design and manufacturing. This factor, I think, makes this plane of particular historic interest among Japanese military aircraft in the Pacific War.

One can trace the origin of "Big Boy" back to the "Oscar" and "Tojo." Yet, the immediate ancestry becomes readily apparent when it is compared with the "Frank" that we looked at a few pages ago. "Frank" was considered one of the very best fighters of the war, but the Ki-87 had all the earmarks of being far better than its predecessor. The war ended before this big plane could be fully tested and readied for production. I wonder if it had been put into production and use, would it have been called "Super Frank."

Upon looking at these photos, probably the first thing that will impress you, as it did the few of us who saw the real thing at Chofu, is the huge size of this bird. After that impact, the rather beautiful design of this plane makes a lasting impression. The Ki-87 is spotted alongside a Nakajima Ki-115 suicide plane, and the farthest one is a Kawasaki Ki-100 "Radial Tony." The latter is a regular size fighter and the size of it compared to that of "Big Boy" gives you an idea of the Ki-87's massiveness.

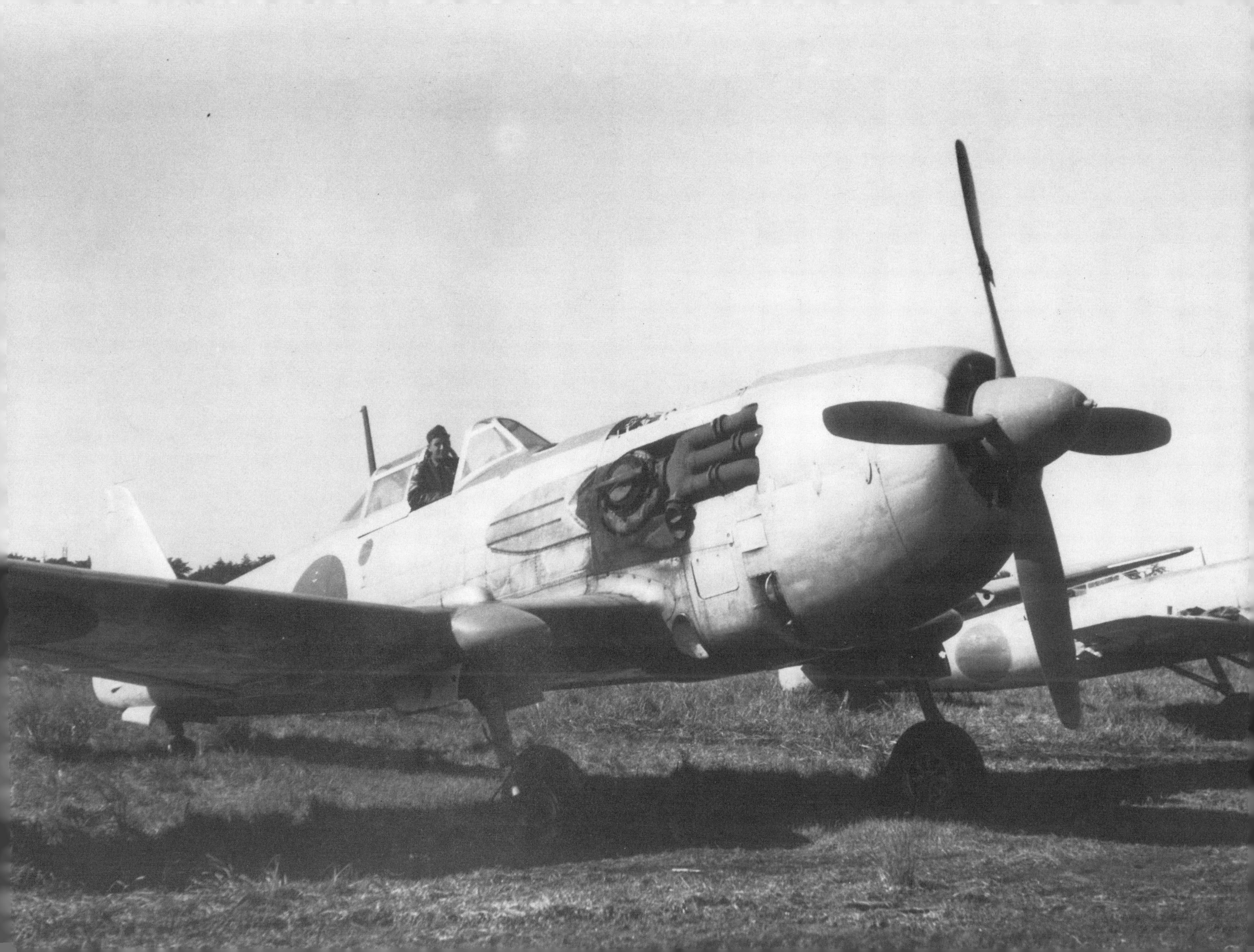

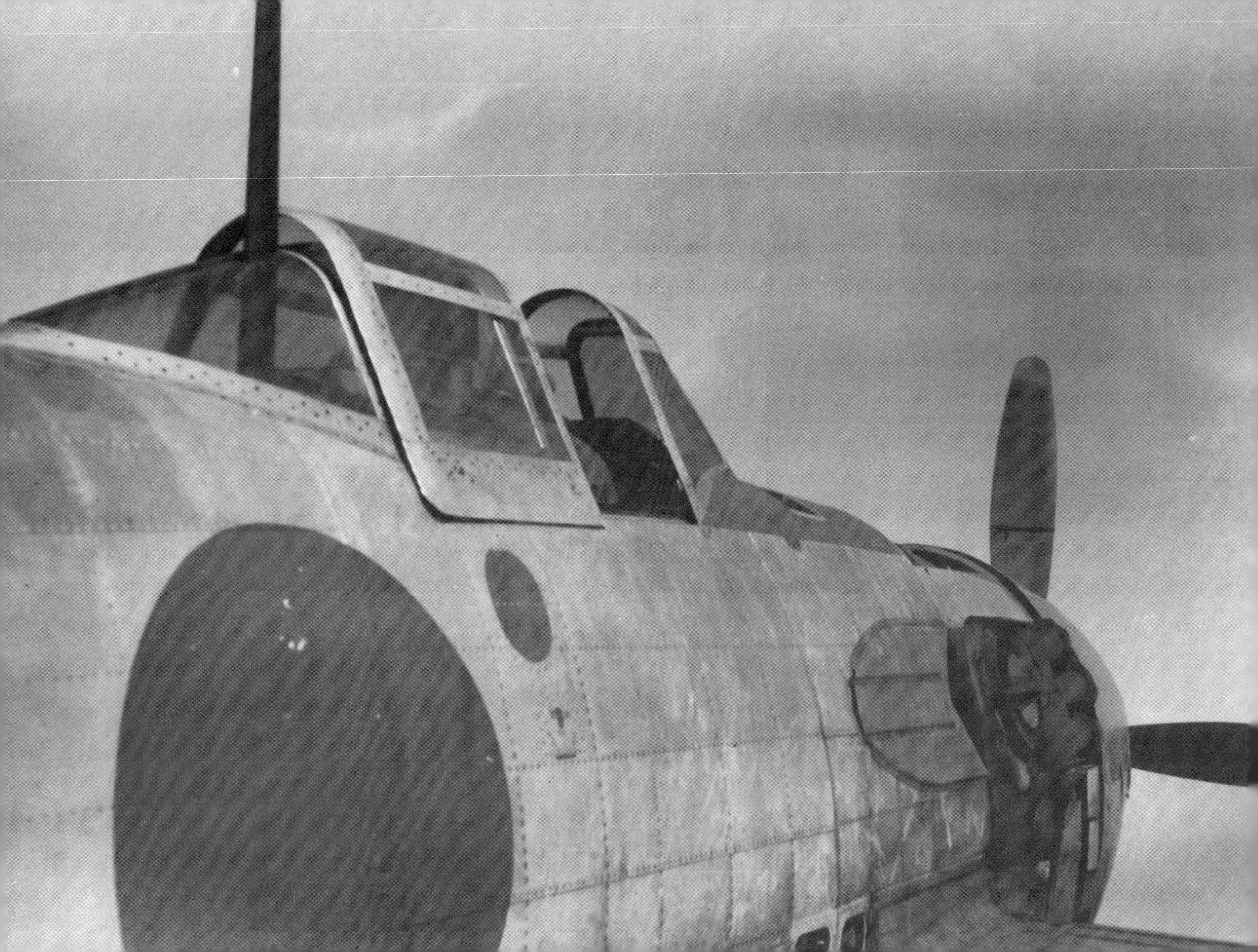

The Nakajima Ki-87: "Big Boy"

I think that the full side view here makes very apparent the relationship of this very impressive looking plane to the famous "Frank."

I feel that there is quite a bit of detail for study in the photos on these pages. The landing gear arrangement is one which reminded me of that of the American P-40. A well for one of the wheels can be seen under the wing, into which, upon retraction, the wheel would swing to the rear while rotating in a ninety degree twist, finally lying flush within the wing. The purpose of this was to give plenty of room in the wings for the installation of cannons and a very large supply of ammunition, with one weapon located between the landing gear and the fuselage, and the other outboard of the landing gear. Probably if you were to see a description of the Ki-87, you would read that the plane was equipped with one 30mm cannon outboard and one 20mm inboard of the landing gear in each wing. Examine the photos here and decide if any guns were carried in this prototype fighter plane. It does not look likely to me, although an empty shell chute can be seen under the wing by the wheel well.

The very large eighteen-cylinder air-cooled radial engine for "Big Boy" was manufactured by Mitsubishi and was said to be rated at 2400 h.p., and it was fronted with a large cooling fan. This sixteen blade fan was geared to move at 150% of the speed of the airscrew. The blades of the fan are quite apparent in the three-quarter front view. Despite all this power aboard, the cowling was beautifully streamlined thanks to the help of the fan. Unlike the smooth, unbroken lines of the port side, the large exhaust-driven supercharger was exposed on the starboard side.

The close-in view gives you more feeling of the size of the Ki-87, and it also affords an opportunity to examine some of the other details. Note the front panel

The Nakajima Ki-87: "Big Boy"

of the windshield. It was made of a bullet-proof glass that was approximately two and a half inches thick, and when I sat in the cockpit and looked through it, everything had a bit of a bluish cast. There was a steel plate behind the pilot's seat for his protection. In standing alongside the fuselage, wonder with me the reason for the small marking in front of the Hinomaru.

Take a look at the dimensions of the Ki-87 compared to those of the P-47, which are stated in the parentheses: span 44 feet (40 feet, 9 inches); length 38 feet, 9 inches (36 feet, 1 inch); height 14 feet, 9 inches (14 feet, 2 inches). "Big Boy" was damn big!

For what it is worth, I have seen only a small handful of pictures of this plane published, and they all look to me like "captured" photos. I think that none have been published, prior to this display, that were taken by an American photographer. So, four more of my pictures are printed on the facing page for all to see.

The photo on page 105 shows 7th Fighter Squadron, 49th Fighter Group P-38 pilot, Lt. Jim Costley of Two Harbors, Minnesota, making his survey from the wing of the Ki-87. Above left is seen a head-on view of this plane that shows clearly the strong dihedral of the wings. Note the big prop that pulled this huge bird through the air at a speed that was said to be well over 425 m.p.h. At left, some 49ers view the plane under the watchful eye of the guard on duty, as the camera views the whole scene from a starboard three-quarter rear angle. Lastly, on the next page, there is a camera study of the front end of "Big Boy"—you take it from there!

Here is a comment on the scarcity of photographs of many things that pertained to the military of wartime Japan. Japan built the largest, and I mean the largest by far, aircraft carrier of the war. In fact, its tremendous size was never even approached until many years after the war when the U.S. Navy launched the so-called super-carriers. This ship was originally started as a battleship, but was, during the intermediate stages of construction, converted into an aircraft carrier. It was named Shinano, and this behemoth had a displacement of between sixty and sixty-five thousand tons. Yet during the war, the U.S. Navy's largest carriers, the Lexington and her sister ship the Saratoga, were thirty-three thousand tons. Shinano was BIG! This huge ship was launched in November of 1944, and was on her initial voyage from Yokosuka headed for the safer waters of the Inland Sea of Japan for completion. On this trip she was torpedoed by the American submarine Archerfish, which had stalked her under the cover of darkness. The Shinano went down on the morning of November 29, 1944.

The point to be made is simply this. I have never seen nor heard of a photograph of Shinano being published—I wonder if there is such a thing as a photo of this ship.

"Peggy" Arrived in Time to Be Too Late!

"Peggy" was the Allied code name assigned to the Japanese Ki-67 Type 4 Heavy Bomber, Hiryu (Flying Dragon). It was designed and manufactured by Mitsubishi for the Japanese Army Air Forces, and it is generally considered to be the finest multi-engine bomber built by that power during the war—only the "Frances" approached it in worth and performance.

While designated as a heavy bomber by the Japanese, when we compare it to its American counterparts, the B-25 and B-26, it must be considered a medium bomber. "Peggy" was built to replace the army bomber, the Mitsubishi Ki-21 "Sally," which had become little more than fighter-fodder.

"Peggy" was first seen in combat in early October of 1944, off Formosa when, in the role of a torpedo plane, it attacked some U.S. fleet units. At the time it was not properly identified, and it was thought to be a new high performance torpedo bomber of the Imperial Navy. History tells us that on some of its missions "Peggy" operated in direct cooperation with the Japanese Navy, and was seen mixed in with JNAF aircraft in attacks against American warships. "Peggy" also served in moderate numbers in the China theatre where it was used as a conventional land attack bomber. The first photos and actual identification of this new plane came from a crashed "Peggy" on the Chinese mainland. Six photos of this crashed plane

"Peggy" Arrived in Time to Be Too Late!

were published in the identification manual, dated December 1944, which was distributed to U.S. air units in the Pacific.

Here is what else was said in that publication (and there was but very little data): "Pilot and co-pilot are protected with 5/8" back and head armor. Strong possibility of radar installation. Fuel tanks leak-proofed with laminated rubber 5/8" thick." Here is what it said about the armament: "Nose 1 12.7mm, top 1 20mm turret, dorsal 2 12.7mm Flex., tail 1 12.7mm turret." The report adds this: "Examination of fin and rudder bear out belief that 'Peggy' is recognitionally somewhat similar to 'Helen'. Remnants of torpedo rack from which a torpedo has been dropped offers the first evidence that torpedo racks have actually been used on an army bomber."

There were the remains of a "Peggy" on Lingayen Airfield on Luzon that I was able to view in February of 1945 and my first impression was that they looked like a trimmed down edition of the "Betty." The capabilities of Japan's aircraft designers must be rated highly, but the construction qualities and the numbers of their aircraft produced could not measure up to American standards. However, from Japanese planes I could observe, "Peggy" came closest to matching the quality of American production multi-engine planes.

If this aircraft type had been on the scene a year sooner, things in the Pacific air war could have been a little different. This plane was far superior to the "Helens," "Sallys," and "Lilys" that were then serving the JAAF. Just under 700 "Peggys" were built, 606 by Mitsubishi and 91 by Kawasaki. Compare this to (in round figures) 5,100 B-26s and 9,500 B-25s—or for that matter 18,000 B-24s that the U.S. produced.

The "Peggys" shown on these pages were photographed at Irumagawa Airbase, which is near Yokota Airbase, Tokyo. I was at that army air base for a couple of days in November, 1945, for the happy duty of being processed for going home, drawing to a close my overseas duty. The photos here are two views of the same "Peggy." This particular one looked like a flying gasoline tanker, with fuel tanks about everywhere. Regarding this plane, what do you think about this rumor that floated around: this "Peggy" was being fitted and readied for the escape of some of Japan's war leaders prior to the arrival of the U.S. Occupation Forces in Japan? Escape to where?

On the following two pages are views of 069 "Peggy" taken inside a rocket and strafe damaged hangar. Like many other of Japan's aircraft types, there were modifications within modifications of "Peggy"—I'll let you readers speculate on this one. At any rate the then very modern, almost jet-age, lines of this Mitsubishi plane are very apparent here.

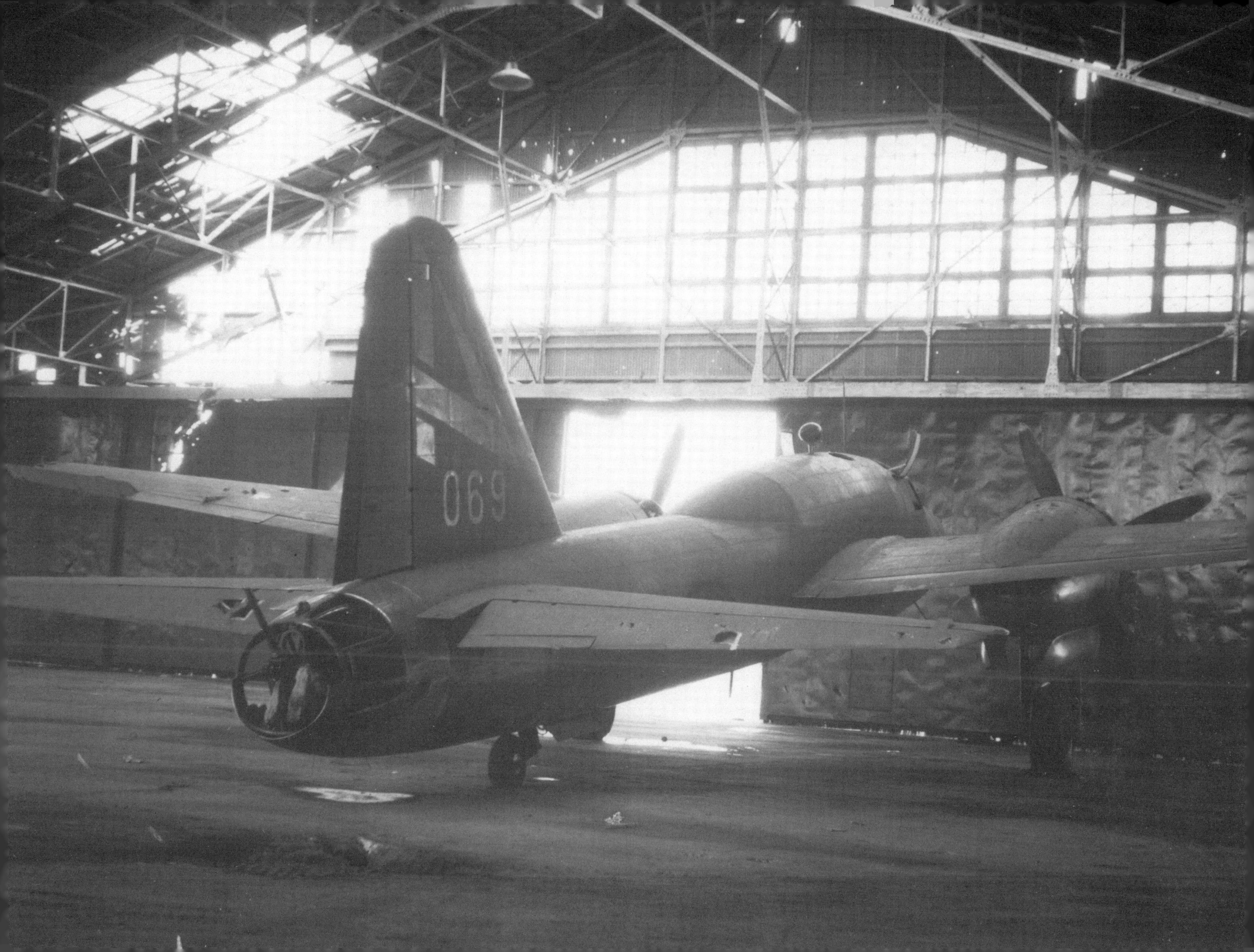
069

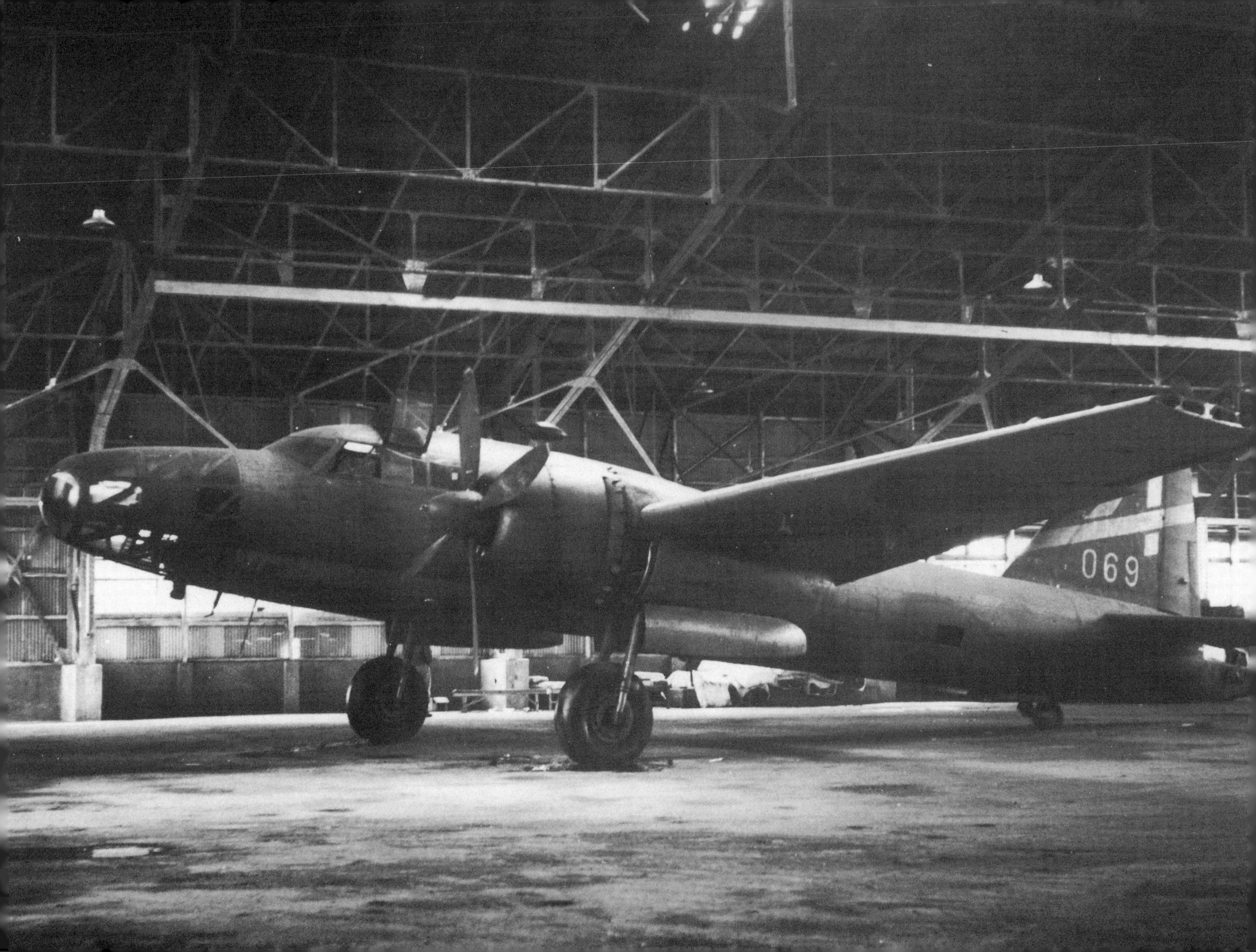
069

"Jacks" Are Better!

When the American forces landed on Leyte in the Philippines in late October of 1944, it was a classic military move. Or should we say military action? At any rate, it triggered one of the greatest reactions in military annals.

These landings at Leyte had the support of the greatest naval power that the U.S. had mustered in the Pacific war up to that time. When the Japanese leaders had definite knowledge of this major attack, the stage became set for the greatest fleet-air engagement ever. The battles for Leyte Gulf were to take place and much has been recounted in writings regarding this epic confrontation of naval might. History has focused these Leyte events into a five or six day span but in doing so has eclipsed another factor that I personally do not think has been adequately expounded in the recounting of the war against Japan. In a sentence let me say this: the struggle for the island of Leyte could almost be compared to the historic Guadalcanal campaign. However the tempo of events that took place at and around Leyte were dramatically faster in execution and even more decisive in results. While the Americans were endeavoring (slowly, but successfully) to secure their positions on the east coast of Leyte, not many miles away on the west coast the Japanese were again and again endeavoring to bolster and reinforce their military strength (sometimes successfully, sometimes not). Also, for many weeks during these times, the American forces had one primitive airfield (maybe two or three if the weather was good, and usually it was not) in operation on Leyte while the Japanese had dozens of airfields on nearby islands, some of which were major airbases.

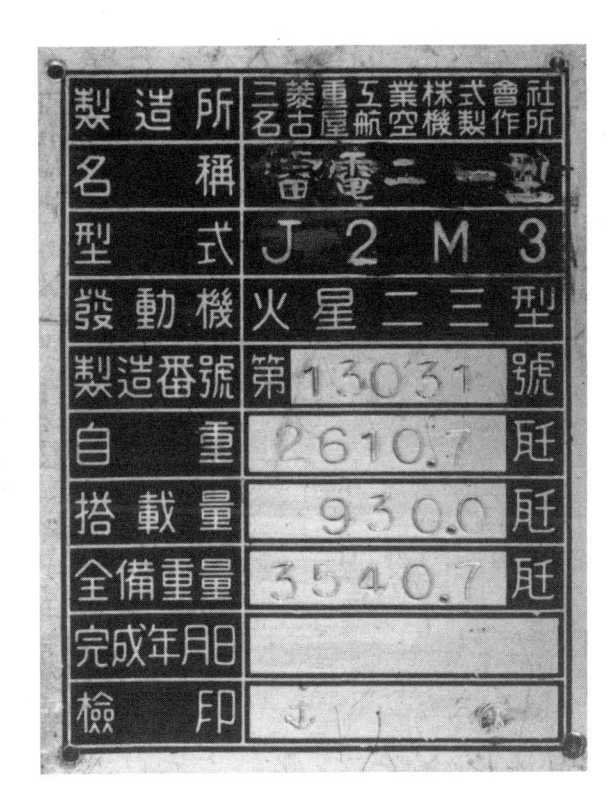

An unusual incident in military events took place on December 7, 1944, when a bold American move took place in an effort to halt these amphibious reinforcements by the Japanese. On the morning of that date American forces made their own "invasion" on the west coast of Leyte about three miles south of Ormoc—and remarkably, only about 40 miles to the north, the Japanese made another reinforcement effort on the same morning. Another air battle was to rage, this time over and around these opposing convoys which brings out the point—namely, "another air battle." While, as was said, Leyte is famous for the sea battles, not very well known is the fact that because of this Philippine Island, a good two months of aerial confrontation continued between the Japanese and U.S. forces. This long campaign also ended in a decisive manner for the Americans.

Through November and December of '44 around the Philippines, the American airmen were seeing several types of Japanese planes that they had not encountered before, and one of these types was a "stocky and sturdy, but fast moving fighter plane." This plane was called "Jack," and I heard nine of the P-38 pilots of the 49th Fighter Group state at the time that this plane was better than any Japanese aircraft they had ever encountered.

I have never seen any factual report on just how many "Jacks" were committed to the Philippines operation by the Japanese Navy Air Force. Despite the relatively small numbers that were used in that theatre, it was the most talked about Japanese plane among the American fighter pilots I knew.

All my photographs of "Jack" were taken at Atsugi in September or early October of 1945. There were about forty of these fighters at that base at the end of the war, and virtually all had been rendered inoperative by the first occupying forces of Americans. A string of nine "Jacks" in the above picture may intrigue that breed of buff who must determine the exact model designation of a given type of aircraft. The natural aluminum finish of the "Jack" on the right is a most unusual one for this navy fighter, as is also the Hinomaru which is surrounded by a large, green band. The foreground plane from the cockpit to the nose is tri-colored, with a dark green anti-glare top surface, while the balance is a medium green with gray-white undersides.

The three "Jacks" in the top photo are among those seen in the preceding photo, only we are a little closer and some modification details become more apparent. I would say that the two nearer planes are the J2M5s, having only two cannons aboard but being equipped with superchargers—these would be the latest production models, made for very rapid climbing speed and high altitude fighting performance. The one in the rear is an earlier model. All have had the aftermost part of the fuselage broken off. On the bottom we get a detailed look at 191, the center plane in the photo above. There is a good bit to see here, and this photograph should fascinate the modeler who likes to take standard plastic kits and devise variations based on pictures of actual aircraft.

Did you ever see a picture of a "Zeke" and a "Jack" side by side giving a comparative idea of size and shape? Check the photo on the following page. Incidentally, the color scheme on this "Jack" is different than the regular run of this plane. The fuselage is of a bright, glossy green with a flat, dark green antiglare area forward of the cockpit. The lower surfaces are of a lustrous white and the propeller hub is painted a sparkling aluminum. If you look at this picture long enough, you will almost feel the transition from the traditional light and highly maneuverable concept of

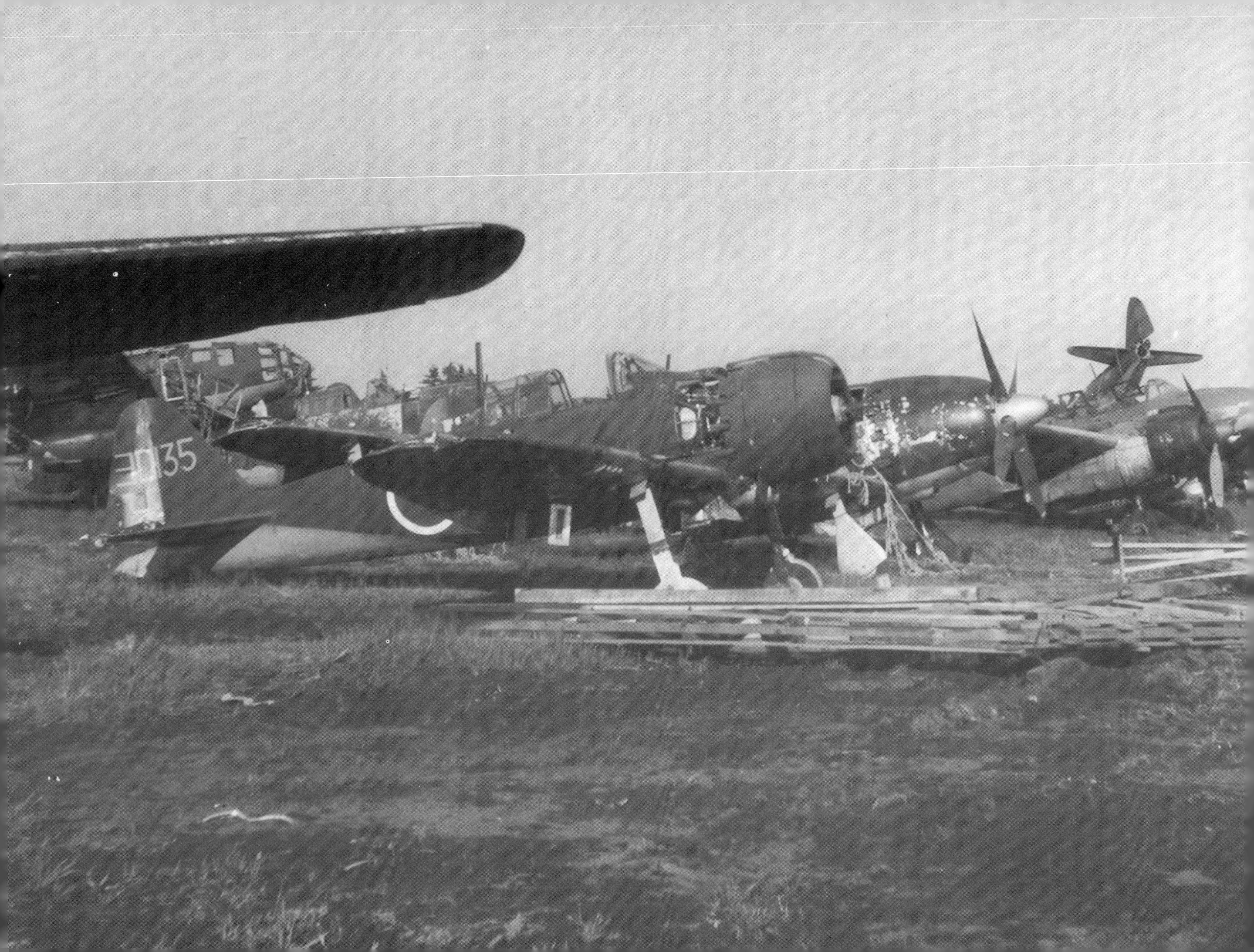
135

the "Zero" into the much more rugged and speed-power factors of the "Jack."

While it was "Jack" to us in the Pacific, this Mitsubishi Navy interceptor-fighter was called Raiden (meaning Thunderbolt) by the Japanese. It was the J2M1, for the first model, on through model J2M5. Japanese sources indicate the production of some 470 Raidens, in all models and variations, up to the end of the war.

In mentally looking at "Jack," several points are certainly noteworthy. For one thing, to the best of my knowledge at least, it was the first navy fighter plane in the war that was designed and produced without equipment for aircraft carrier operations. More particularly, this plane was designed and built as an interceptor fighter on a local area basis—its range was notably shorter than other Japanese fighter craft. It was first tested in 1942, and got into only very limited production in the months that followed. It was an example of excellence in concept and design, not being matched by the hard-pressed technology, production facilities, and material supplies of the Japanese aircraft industry.

This land-based navy fighter's power plant was one of over 1800 h.p., with fourteen cylinders, swinging a big, four-bladed prop. In order to streamline this plane with all of this horsepower in a radial engine, an engine-driven fan was installed in front to force more air in for cooling purposes. A very large spinner on the propeller enhanced the frontal aspects of this fighter's lines, both aerodynamically and aesthetically.

And the total aspects of "Jack" were very different from the traditional Japanese fighter plane. For the first time aerial gymnastics—more properly, high maneuverability—was not the prime factor to be considered. "Jack" was conceived along the latest western ideals of a fighter plane, having a good degree of sturdiness, high diving speeds, and very fast climbing abilities—and just plain old speed! Armor plate was installed behind the pilot's seat in all of the many "Jacks" I saw, and, although most of these fighters were armed with four 20mm cannons, some had two, while a few had the striking power of six cannons. The late model "Jacks," fitted with superchargers, have been rated as Japan's best bomber interceptor of the war—the best anti-B-29 weapon of all.

Interestingly, "Jack" is the only standard combat plane of Japan that I have never heard of (or read about) being used in suicide attacks upon ships.

Wonder with me awhile what might have happened if the Mitsubishi J2M "Thunderbolt" ever had a run in with the Republic P-47 "Thunderbolt." It might be mentioned that there was also another pair of names for planes either similar or of the same designation. They are Britain's Hawker "Hurricane" and the Nakajima Ki-84 ("Frank") Hayate. I have seen Hayate translated in some writings as gale and in other descriptions as hurricane. At any rate, there is a very good possibility that there was a clash of the "Thunderbolts!"

I am including three pages of intelligence data. This information was gathered and compiled up to the end of 1944 and describes the earlier production planes, probably the type most used in the Philippines. This intelligence material also lets us know that "Jacks" are better!

Praise must be given to the work of the Air Force Intelligence people during the war in the Pacific—the work that these men did was truly outstanding, but unfortunately, although I am sure properly, remained unheralded at the time. I personally salute them now, because my small role of being a Squadron Communications Officer then gave me an opportunity to gain an insight into their extremely important contributions to the whole thing out there.

JACK 11

105A-2

AIRCRAFT

Duty	Fighter
Designation	(RAIDEN) Model 11
Description	Low-wing Monoplane
Mfg.	Mitsubishi
Engines	1 Crew 1
Construction	All metal

ENGINES

	H.P.	Altitude
Take-off	1870	S.L.
Normal	1370	9,850'
Military	1580	S.L.
	1560	17,900'
War Emerg.	1940	4,400'

Mfg. Mitsubishi
Model KASEI 23
Type Radial
Cylinders 14   Cooling Air
Supercharger 2 Speed
Propeller 4 blade C.S.diam. 10.8'
Fuel—Take-off 92   Cruising 92 plus methanol

DIMENSIONS

Span 35.4'   Length 31.8'
Height 12.9' Wing area 216 sq. ft.

PERFORMANCE AND CHARACTERISTICS

TAKE-OFF

	Load	Feet
T.O. calm	7080	585
T.O. 25 kt. wind	7080	261
T.O. over 50' obstacle		
Landing over 50' obstacle		

CLIMB—CEILING

@ 7080	lbs.	Feet	Min.
Rate @ S.L.		4600	1
Rate @ 14,800 ft.		4080	1
Time to 10,000'			2.6
Time to 20,000'			5.6
Service ceiling 37,500'			

SPEED

	Mph.	Knts.	Altitude
Maximum	350	304	@ S.L.
Maximum	407	355	@ 17,400'
Cruising 75%	228	197	1,500'
Economical			

BOMBS—CARGO

	No.	Size	Total Lbs.
Normal	None		
Maximum	2 x	35 kg.	154

WEIGHTS

	Lbs.
Empty	5178
Gross	7080
Overload	8045

FUEL

	U.S. gal.	Imp. gal.
Built-in	109	90
Internal (Removable)	48	40
External (drop)	66	55
Maximum	223	185

RANGE AND RADIUS

	Miles		Speed		Alt. feet	Fuel gal.		Bombs lbs.	Cargo lbs.
	stat.	naut.	mph.	Knts.		U.S.	Imp.		
Maximum range (maximum fuel) At 75% Vmax.	1127	968	156	135	1500	223	185	154	None
Maximum range (normal fuel) At 75% Vmax.	912	795	208	180	1500	223	185	154	None
	650	564	165	143	1500	109	90	None	None
Radius ( )	508	440	228	197	1500	109	90	None	None
Radius ( )									

GENERAL DATA

JACK is cleanly designed. The fact that it has a short range and high rate of climb indicates that it will be used as an interceptor fighter. It can carry a small bomb under each wing which will probably be employed for air to air attack against bomber formations.

Wing fuel tanks are not used under Gross Load. A jettisonable belly tank and 2 x 35 kg external bombs are allowed for under "Maximum Range".

DATE December 1944

RESTRICTED

"Jacks" Are Better! 119

JACK 11
FIELDS OF FIRE

105A-3

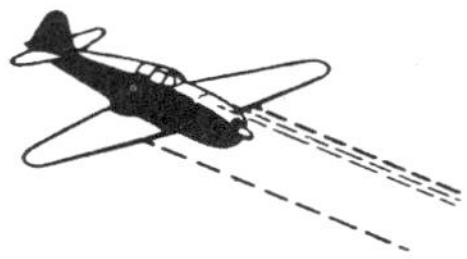

FORWARD GUNS "A" AND "B"
¾-front view from above

EXHAUST FLAME PATTERNS

REAR VIEW

VULNERABILITY

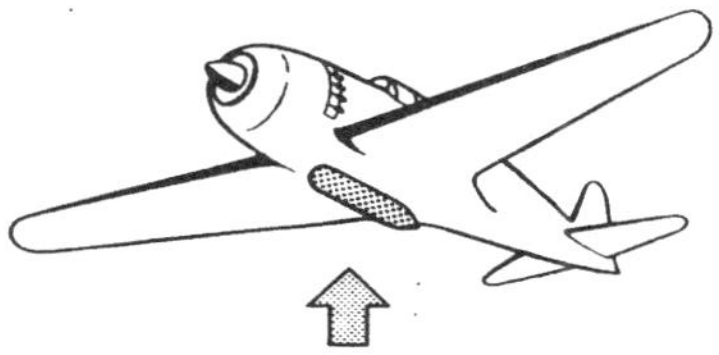

OXYGEN

FORWARD GUN "B"
1 x 20 mm.

FORWARD GUN "B"
1 x 20 mm.

FORWARD GUNS "A"
2 x 7.7 mm.

Auxiliary gas tank Jettisonable

LEGEND
- Fuel tanks, unprotected
- Fuel tanks, protected
- Oil tanks, unprotected
- Oil tanks, protected

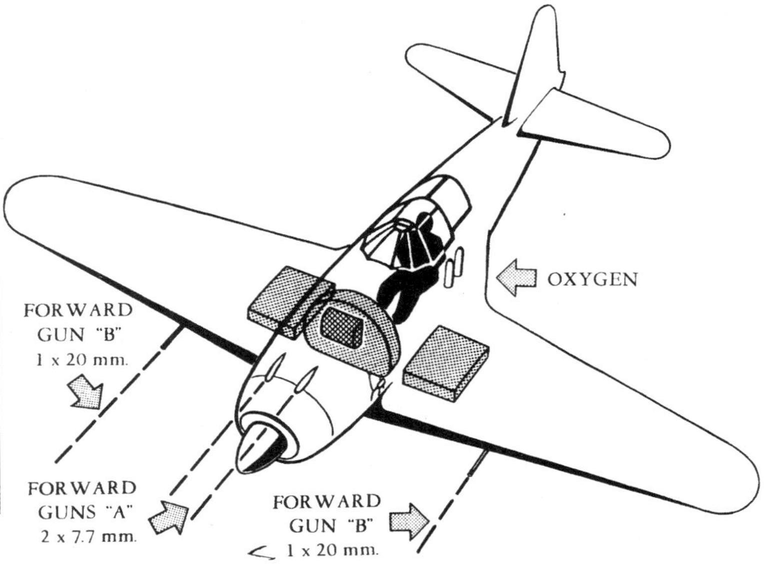

ARMAMENT

	No.	Size	Rds. Gun	Type		No.	Size	Rds. Gun	Type
Forward	4 or 2	20 mm 7.7mm	100 550	Fixed Fixed	Tail				
Top and	2	20 mm	100	Fixed	Wing				
Side									
Bottom									

TACTICAL DATA

JACK is more powerful and heavily armed than previous Japanese fighters. Probably less maneuverable than ZEKE but superior in diving and climbing at high speeds.

No armor or fuel protection have been indicated.

DATE December 1944

RESTRICTED

120 "Jacks" Are Better!

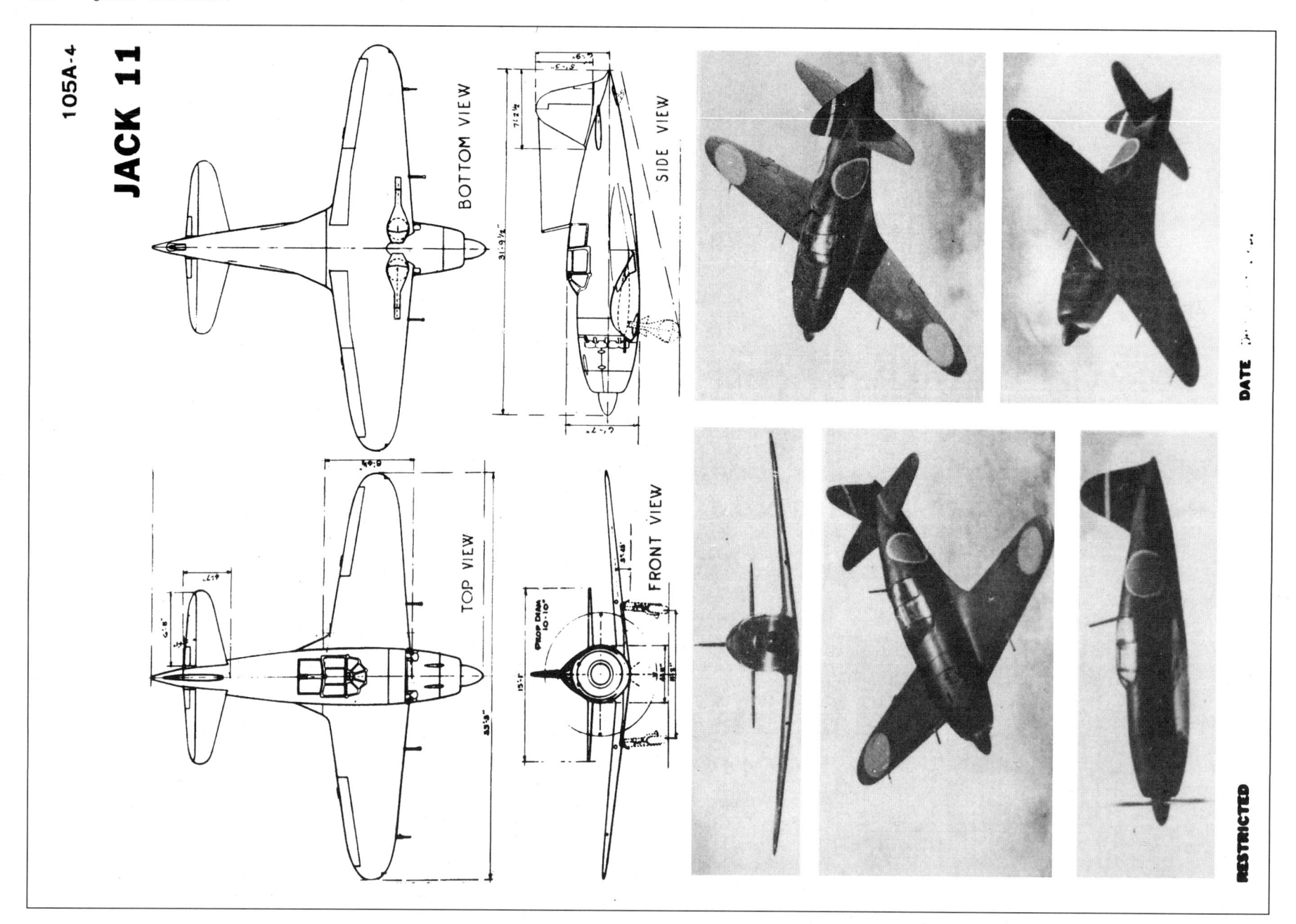

A "Jack" Is "Captured" by the 49th Fighter Group

What would you do if you were an "old" Southwest Pacific veteran who had served your time, the war was now over, you were with the first occupation forces in Japan and now you were due to go home any day soon—and you are a part owner of a "Jack"? You'd have done the same damn thing I did, get a friend to take your camera and get a shot of you in the cockpit. Jim Costley, seen in the photo on page 105, did the taking, and there I sit looking like the owner or something—maybe more like Manfred von Groundpounder.

Among the very first occupation forces in Japan were many Air Force men (excluding the aircrews) who should have been sent home long ago. A point system had been devised, the count of which was based on months in the service, months in overseas duty, campaigns, awards, and so forth. But the need to maintain the very high efficiency of many units for the coming invasion of Japan had compelled our "leaders" to keep very many men well past their time of going back to The States. However, after the initial occupation moves into Japan went surprisingly well, the people in charge wasted no time in getting the

have these photos you see here of that plane. Somehow, these are my most valued photos of all the Japanese airplane pictures that I took.

These pictures of "Jack" will be displayed with a little comment, but no captions—a little background should be given. It was in late September of '45 at Atsugi, and each day would see fewer and fewer intact Japanese planes of the hundreds that were there. And each day the boneyards of wrecked planes were becoming larger. Some of us of the 49th would watch the field being cleared to make room for the U.S. airpower. Many types of Japanese Navy aircraft were being literally shoved aside and rent, yet no one at the time thought much about it—after all these had been war weapons that had been used against us.

Not only the pilots of the 49th, but also the ground crewmen admired the design and the quality of "Jack" more than any other standard Japanese plane they had seen. They felt that there was a certain rugged beauty in this particular type of aircraft. So, spontaneously it happened, a "Jack" must be saved and then restored to ready status—after all, the occupation was a secure thing now and what was wrong with having another kind of plane in the group besides the P-38s? As one crewchief joked, "MacArthur doesn't have to know about it." Over at one edge of the field there was a "Jack" in a revetment that was only superficially rendered inoperative. This was the one to be "captured!"

A small band of the 49th ground crewmen was formed without any leadership or authority, they got a volunteer bulldozer operator and went to work. A "Jack" was soon to be in safe hands.

The "Jack" was placed within an unfinished hangar that was about a hundred yards away from the hangar where the 49th Fighter Group's shops and

"old men" out and home. Still there was one catch—you could walk up the gangplank of the troopship home with only what you could carry. I could manage two barracks bags.

So things being the way they were, I had to leave much that I "owned" behind. When I walked down the gangplank of the U.S.S. General Randall at Tacoma, in November of 1945, I was comfortably carrying only one not-too-full barracks bag. I left a trail on the ocean of odds and ends of clothes and stuff along the great circle route from Yokohama to Washington State. I was now traveling light. In that one bag there was a good number of rolls of exposed 120 film which I was to develop soon after I arrived home. Most of what was on that film is shown in this book. I did not have any parts of the "Jack," but I did

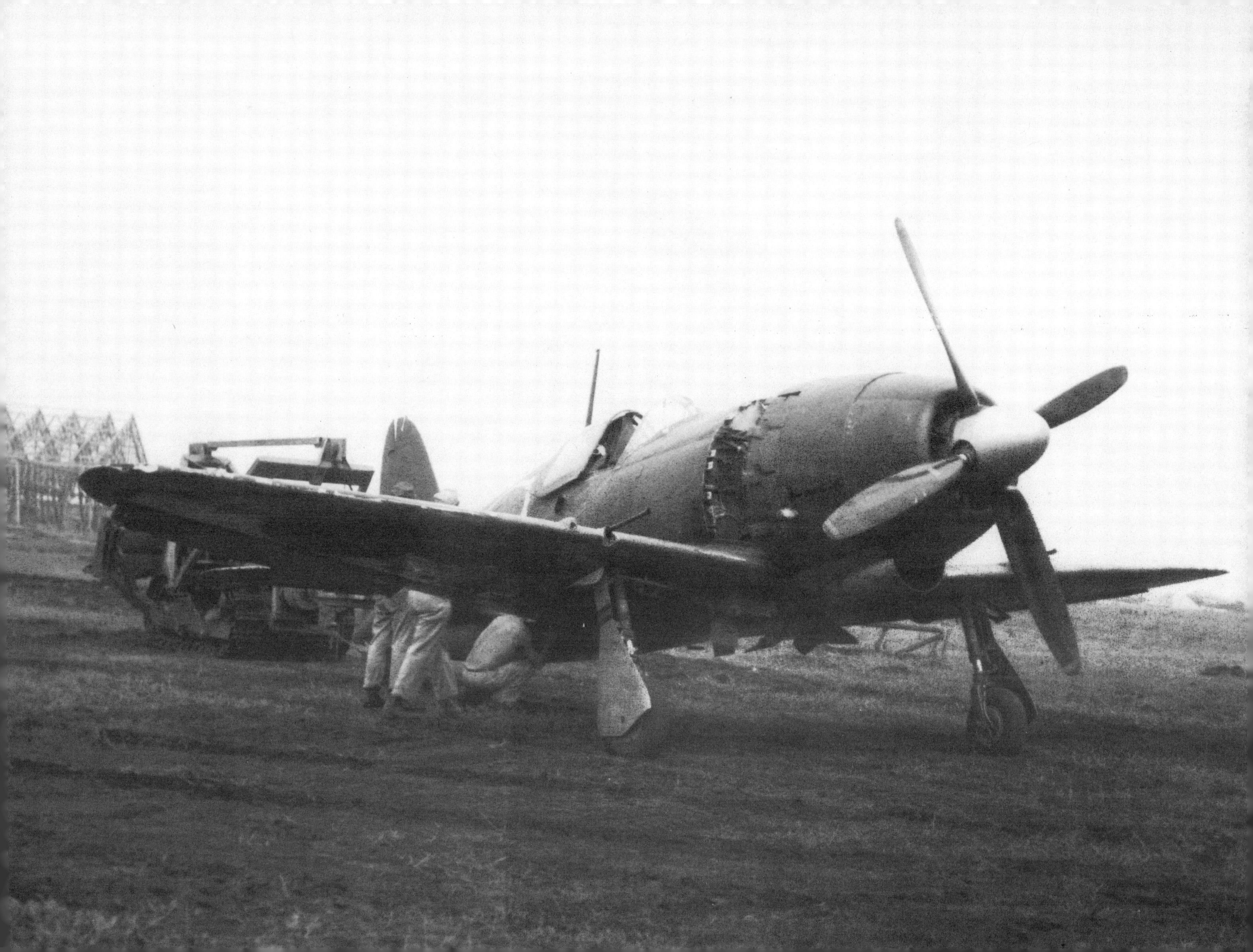

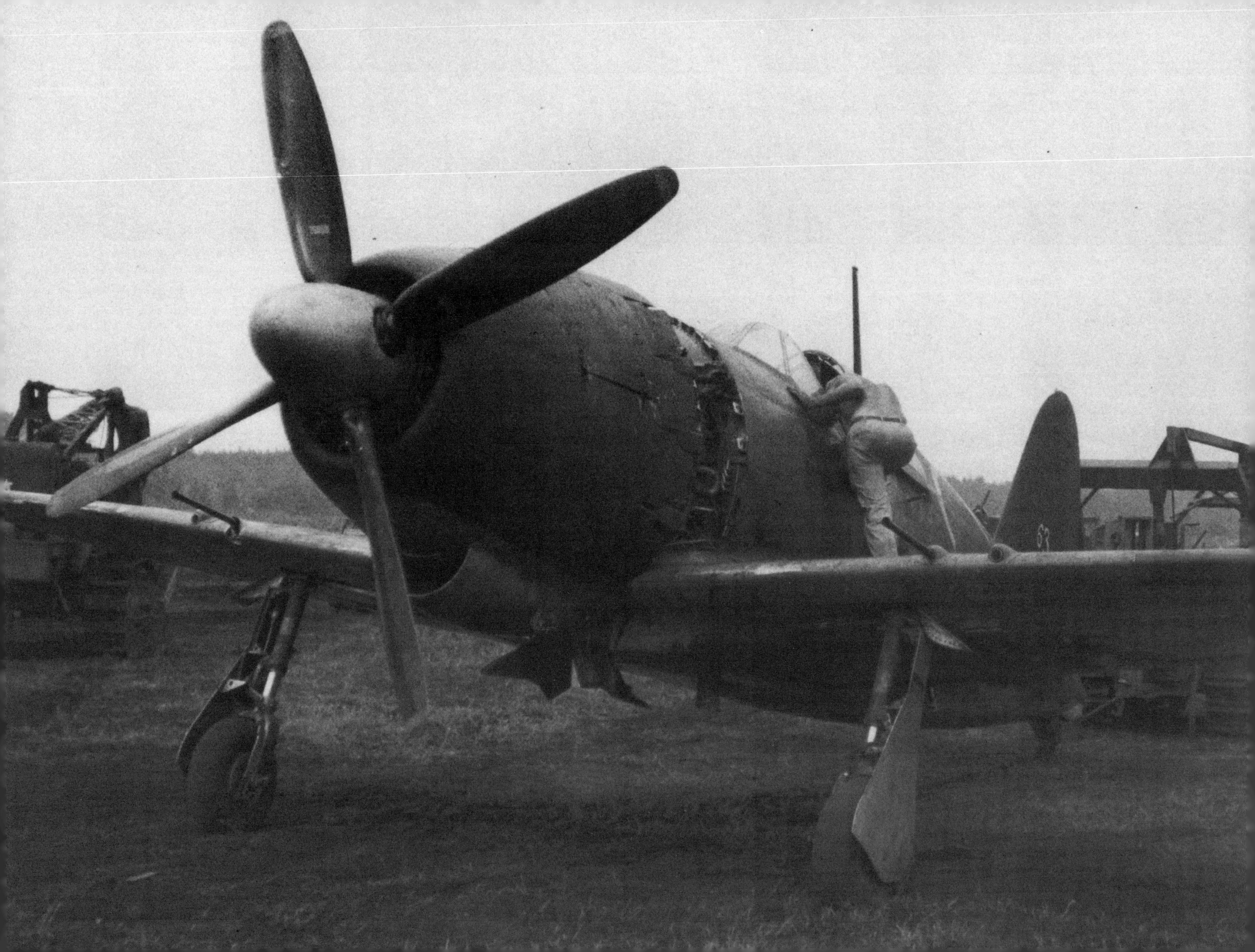

equipment were located. Phase one was now complete—"Operation Save a Jack" was a success.

The next step was to be the restoration of the plane—there were plenty of planes around for the parts. Some of the necessary items were gathered up and stored in the Group's hangar and some of the work on the 49th Fighter Group's "Jack" was getting started. Was the job ever finished? Did the 49th's "Jack" remain "saved?"

In October '45, men were being sent home by the numbers and soon I was too. I don't know the answers to those questions. Do any of you readers?

These photos are of the 49th Fighter Group's "Jack." I must confess that I am certainly glad that I took them. Now it is my hope that you enjoy seeing and examining them.

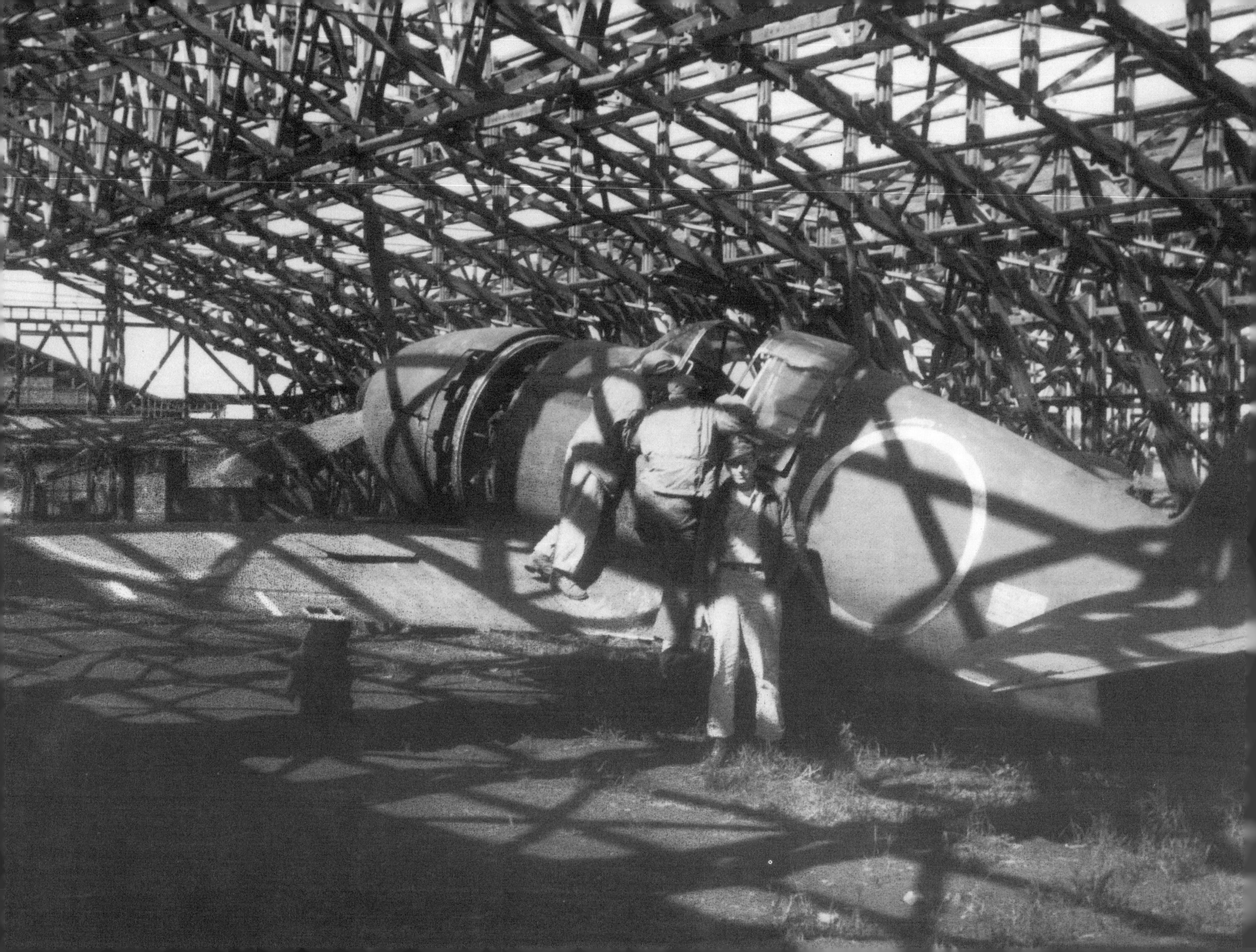

The Last Roundup

The scenes on these pages are to me unforgettable: look at them awhile yourself and they may well be unforgettable for you, too. Although all of these were taken at Atsugi, there were the same type of events going on at other airfields of Japan. These scenes are indicative of the final crushing, literally, of Japanese military airpower.

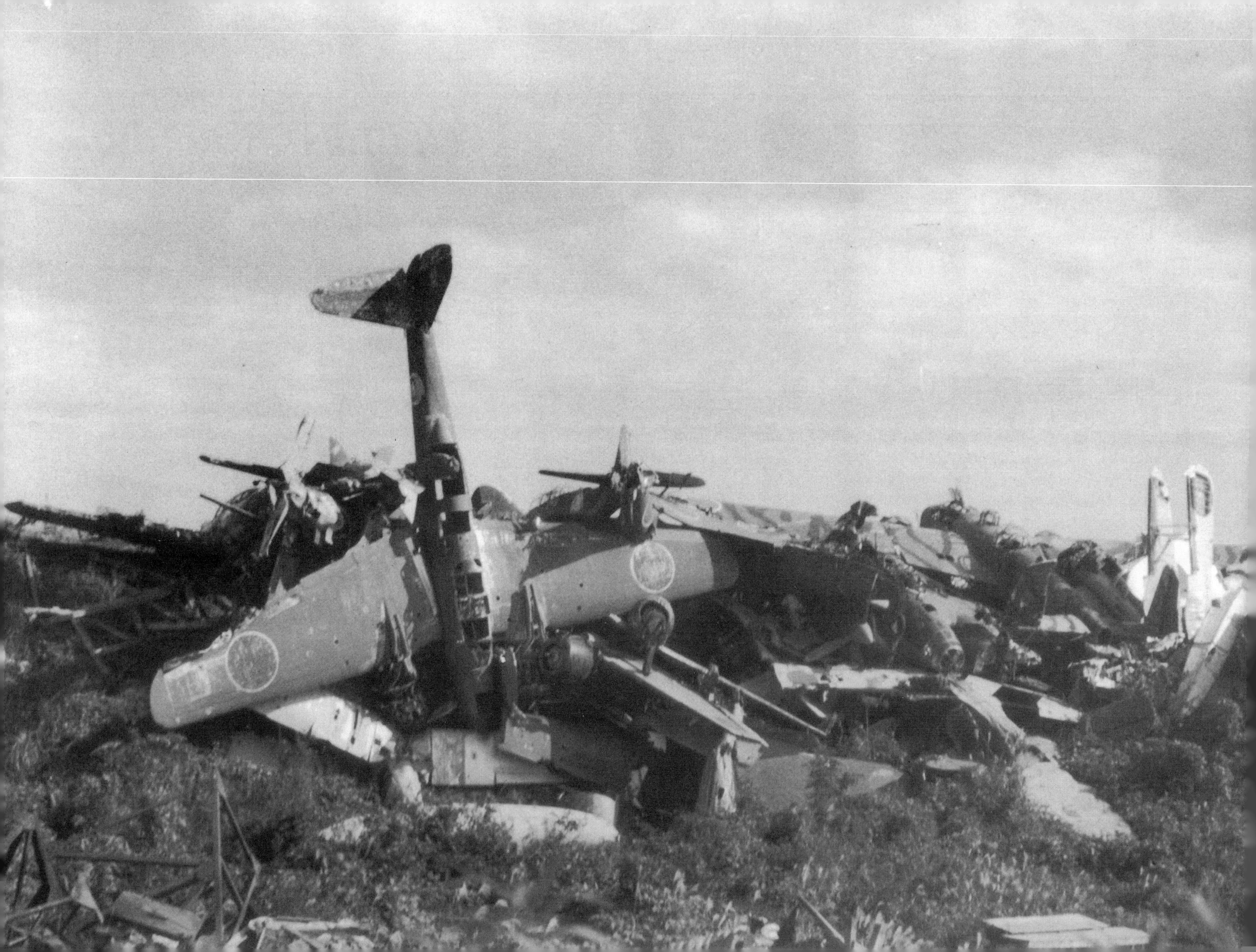

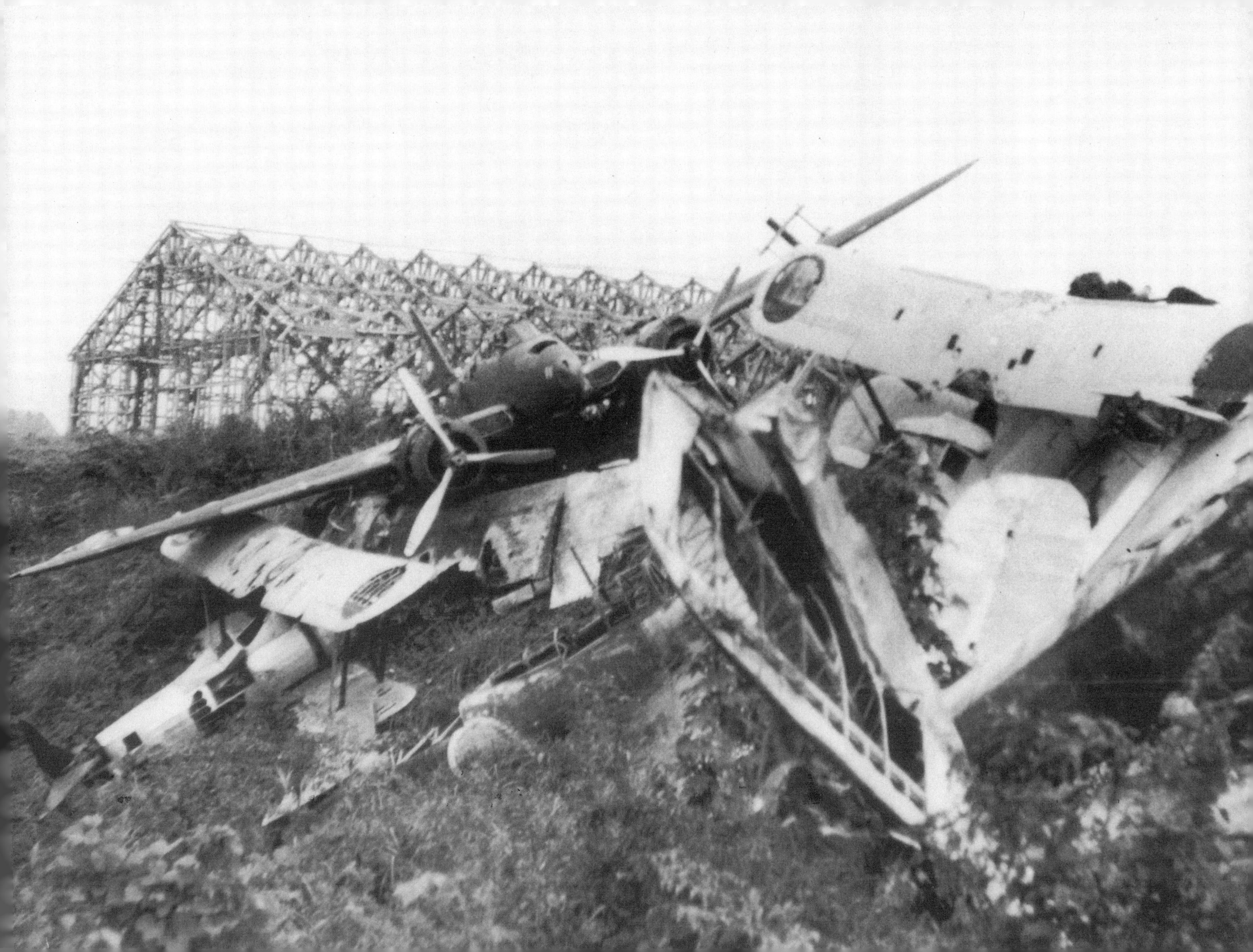

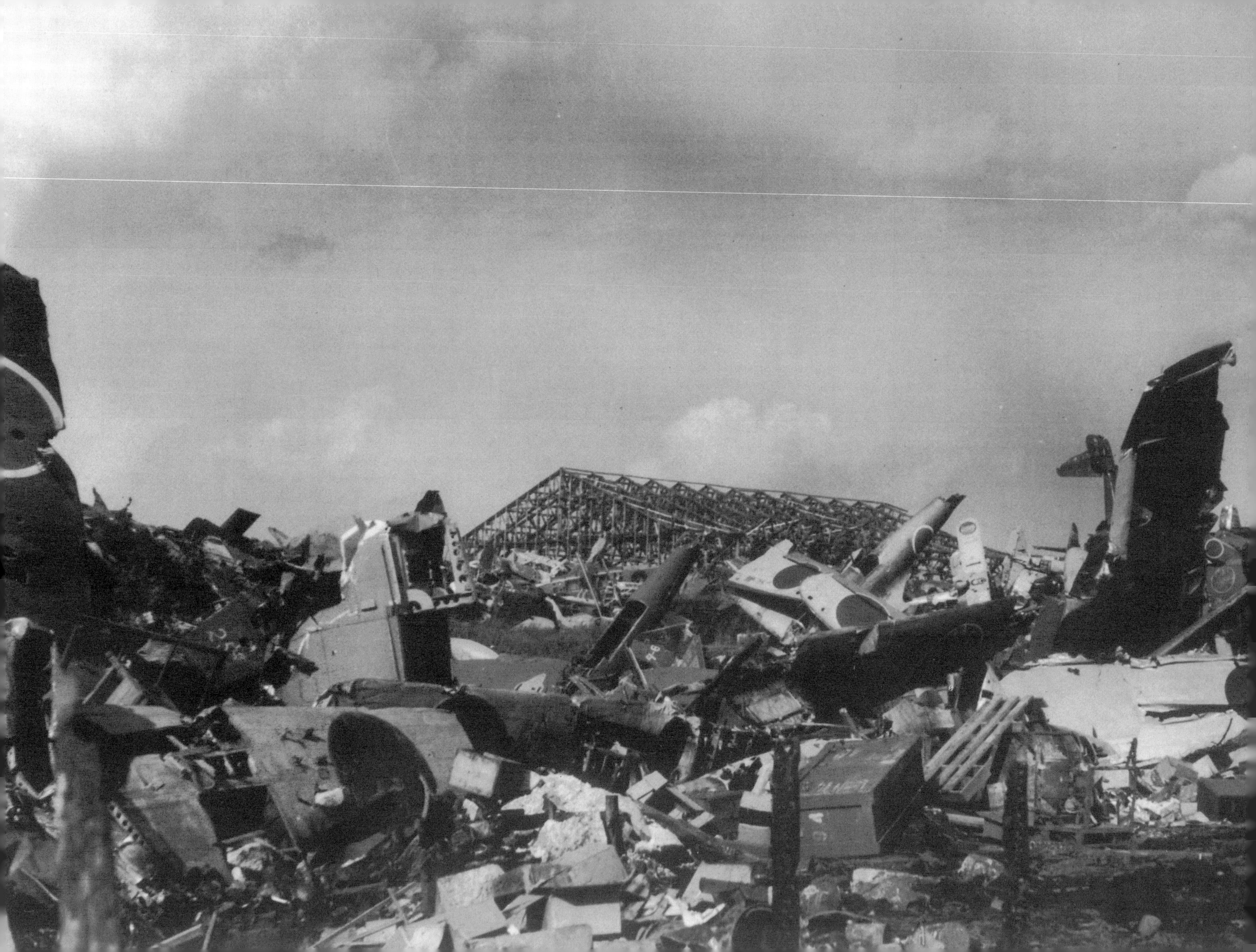

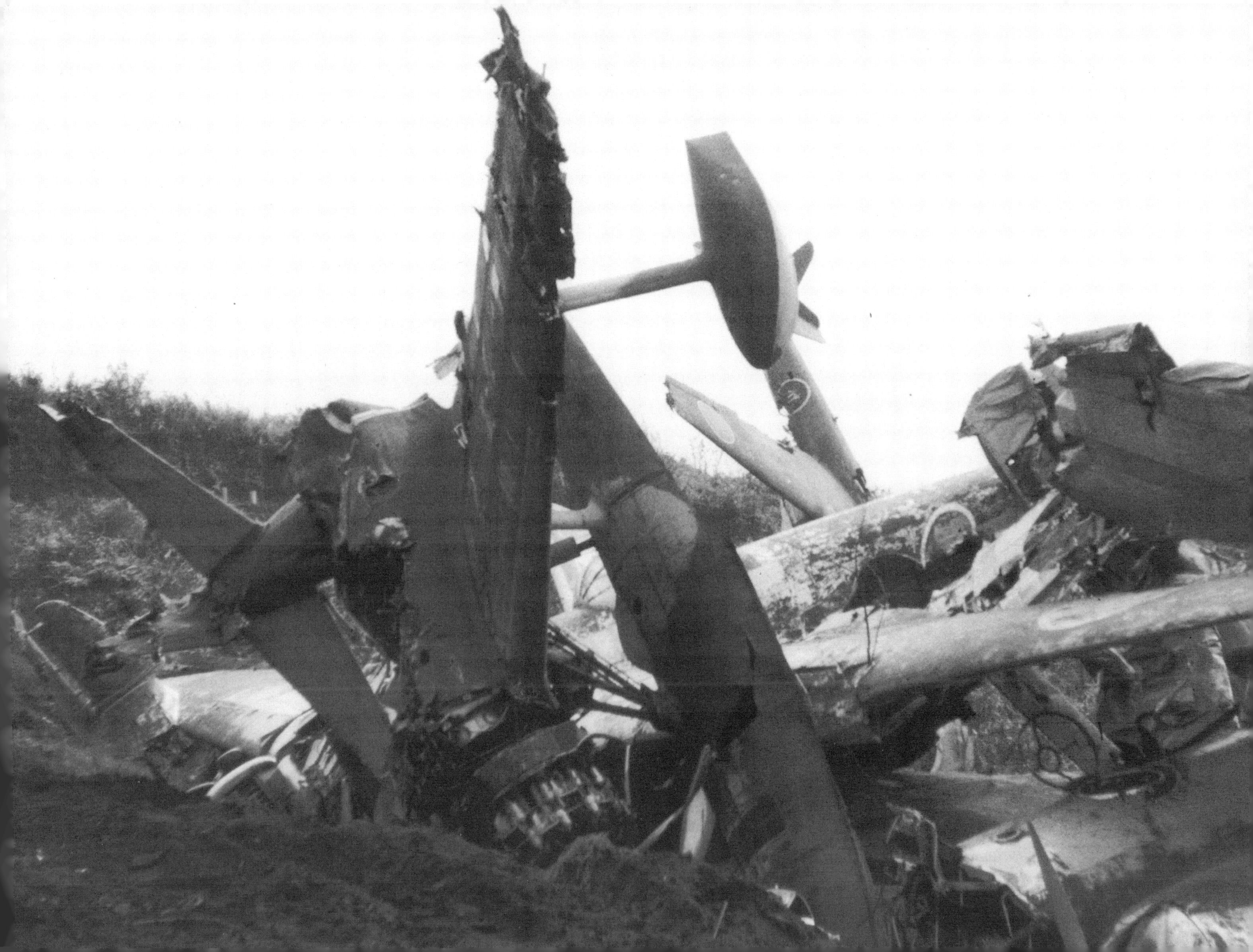

Random Remarks

When I arrived at Milne Bay at easternmost New Guinea in October of 1943, I had been in uniform for just a year, but now the Pacific War had become a more personal event. At the time I was a member of the 33rd Fighter Control Squadron and we now had become a part of the Fifth Air Force. I had read about Milne Bay before and that location should have a very important place in World War II history, although the reason why may well be generally forgotten now. The Japanese had landed a force there and, after several days of bitter fighting, were defeated with remnants "driven into the sea." It was the first Japanese landing to be defeated, which event signaled the end of the forward motion of their expansion in that theatre of war. Several wrecked Japanese landing-barges still remained on one of the beaches along with live ammunition and other equipment in the water just off shore. The battle had taken place in August of 1942 and now, a year later, Milne Bay was a forward staging and supply area for the Australian and American forces. Most of the area was like a black mud hole, very hot and humid, and smelling of jungle decay.

It was here that my knowledge of geography was to start to expand. Being in New Guinea now, about the first thing I was to learn came from 1) living (?) experience, 2) the common consent of the men who had been there, 3) looking at a large map of that second largest island of the world—Milne Bay was the hole of New Guinea. Besides that, it was an awful long way from home, and a hell of a long way to Tokyo.

Further study of a map of the Pacific, showing the bases we had (damn few) and those the Japanese had (too damn many), made most of us believe and feel, and I say this with all sincerity, that we would not see home for a good five years. Even with this in mind, winning of the war was just kind of taken for granted. Yet I was to be riding around Tokyo in a jeep less than two years later. Now, how did this happen so fast? Put another way, how did victory come so relatively soon? The complete answer to this might well take ten volumes, but in a sentence maybe this is the answer. Our country, the U.S., was totally involved in the resolve and effort to crush the (then) enemy completely—and that it did with the help of its Allies.

Now, the Japanese Air Forces had led the way in the early conquests of the Land of the Rising Sun. In order to reverse these victories of Japan, the neutralization and destruction of that country's air power always remained foremost in the plans of the Allied leaders. The culmination of these neutralization efforts came with the basing of B-29s on the Marianas Islands having as their prime target the destruction of the aircraft industry of Japan. These attacks at the source of aircraft manufacturing are generally well known by those familiar with the history of the Pacific War.

Let me mention some things that, while not as "final" as the B-29 strikes at the source, still were effective enough to "chip away" at Japan's airpower. This attrition of Japanese airpower was enough to permit the location of B-29 bases close enough to the

Home Islands to be practical. Certainly worthy of note is the U.S. Navy's heavy anti-aircraft gun known as the 5 inch 38. It fired a shell that was equipped with what was called a proximity fuse. The projectile would explode instantly as it passed within approximately sixty feet of the magnetic field of the target, the enemy aircraft. It would detonate into a black cloud of destruction, ripping the air with deadly steel fragments. This then-secret weapon took a significant toll of attacking Japanese planes. It first went into use in late 1942 in the Solomons campaign, and was to become standard equipment on larger U.S. warships.

Another well-kept secret during the war was the breaking of Japan's military communications code. Because of this advantage, the Battle of Midway resulted in a disastrous blow to Japan's airpower. Japan's "surprise" attack against Midway was no surprise at all.

Australian coast watchers, scattered through some of the South Pacific islands, often gave more than an hour's advance notice of approaching Japanese aircraft and this allowed the maximum effective use of defensive fighter interception and anti-aircraft readiness. In New Guinea, New Britain, and the Solomons, there were even, at times, some dauntless Aussie "bushmen" spotted in the hills overlooking some of the major Japanese airbases. By means of their portable radio transmitters, the Allies were able to get information on the deployment of some of Japan's aircraft.

An important factor that was to contribute to the downfall of Japan's air arm was the use of the submarine. American subs would hit at shipping along the supply lanes of Japan, depriving its forward bases of fuel, parts, and equipment—fuel was even to become scarce at Japan's Home Islands, restricting the training of pilots and aircrews.

Photo-reconnaissance planes of the U.S., both army and navy, would often make daring penetration flights over enemy-held territory. Knowledge gained from these missions would enable the Allies to react with carefully planned attacks at shipping and airfields at the right times and places. Thus squadrons of Japanese planes were crippled or wrecked on the ground by bold airfield assaults, initiated because of effective air reconnaissance.

Allied planes were equipped with an electronic device called IFF (meaning identification friend or foe). These small "block boxes," installed on each plane, sent certain coded pulsations that were picked up by radar. Radar-screen scans, whose targets showed no IFF signals, were immediately called "bogies," which meant unidentified aircraft. If positively identified as hostile aircraft, the term was replaced with the word "bandit." Because of this IFF device, surprise raids of Japanese aircraft were kept at a minimum and, because of the IFF and radar, controlled intercept missions could be run and anti-aircraft batteries would be on full alert, whether at sea or on land. It should be noted here that Allied development and use of radar was years ahead of the Japanese, who had none in use during the first year or so of the war.

The U.S. Navy, to bolster its task forces against air attacks, had some cruisers, and even battleships, made into virtual floating anti-aircraft bases. These vessels took a heavy toll of Japanese aircraft that got through the combat air patrols or the intercept scrambles.

Land-based, radar-controlled 90mm heavy anti-aircraft guns made even night attacks by high level bombers a hazardous occupation for Japanese aircrews. Among others, I remember one particular night raid on Cape Gloucester, New Britain in early February of 1944. Seven Rabaul-based twin-engine bombers made an attack and three were definitely destroyed (with an additional probable) by sharp shooting Marine 90mm anti-aircraft gunners.

By 1944, after a slow start in effectiveness, specialized night fighter squadrons, with radar-equipped planes, had become an element of defense that reaped a harvest of intruding Japanese aircraft. The Navy used primarily the single-engine Grumman F6F "Hellcat," while the AAF was using the Northrop P-61 "Black Widow," a big twin-engine fighter, during the last year of the war.

Fighter Control Squadrons, units that have never received any fame for the essential work that they performed so well, coordinated Air Force operations and the Signal Corps radar, along with Anti-Aircraft Artillery, into so-called Fighter Sectors. These were the communication centers in each combat area where all pertinent information came in. The continuous information, worked on the plotting boards (comprised of the local area map), made for a team endeavor of the radar, anti-aircraft, and the fighter squadron intercept flights. Coastwatcher reports (regarding enemy aircraft) and even intercepted Japanese radio messages ended here with the Controller, the officer on duty in charge of the Fighter Sector. Because of the quick establishment of these information centers, and the capable use of them, it was very seldom that an air raid was not a costly affair in planes and aircrews for the attacking Japanese.

There were other factors that added to the demise of the Japanese Air Forces as an effective counter to the progress of the Allies in the Pacific, but none will ever be more romanticized, talked about, or written about than the fighter pilot and the fighter plane.

I was to get a bit of an education regarding both in early October 1944, when I was transferred from the 33rd Fighter Control Squadron. I left Middleburg Island, which is off Cape Sansapor, the northernmost part of Western New Guinea, and joined the 49th Fighter Group at Biak Island. From this base, the 49th made its next move . . . to the Philippines. When we landed at Leyte, I was assigned to the 7th Squadron of that Group as its Communications Officer.

At that time the 49th was loaded with aces, including Dick Bong (America's greatest ace), Jerry R. Johnson, Bob DeHaven, Joel Paris, Frenley Damstrom. There were dozens of others and they were all flying the Lockheed P-38 "Lightning," the type of aircraft that is credited with downing more Japanese aircraft in aerial combat than any other Allied plane. The 49th had earlier been a P-40 outfit, a plane in which they scored many of their victories. But now, as a P-38 group, it was the most formidable fighter group in the Pacific, and possibly the world. The 49th closed out with a score of 676 confirmed victories in aerial combat, and a large number of unconfirmed wins. That was the highest score in the Pacific War for any group.

On the following page is seen a 7th Squadron P-38 as viewed from under the tail surfaces of another "Lightning." This scene was taken at Atsugi in late September of 1945 and there is a feeling of quiet and peace. To me, this photo reflects the end of the career of a great airplane. In the hands of a fine pilot, it was a superb fighter plane and, in the hands of a good pilot, it was a great airplane destroyer.

While P-38s of the 49th were the early warbirds at Atsugi, by October, 1945, the place was getting crowded with Allied planes—mostly American aircraft of various models. An idea of this gathering of planes can be seen in the preceding photo. And speaking of Atsugi, it was at this major Japanese airbase, in the Tokyo-Yokohama area, that the initial occupation forces of the Allies landed—and it was here, too, that General Douglas MacArthur first set foot on the soil of Japan.

The next photo is to be the last one for this book and it is one that, somehow, I find myself looking at again and again. Taken in September of 1945, it projects, I think, the great expanse of Atsugi Naval Air Station. To the left in the photo can be seen the south end of the mile-long paved airstrip and its parallel taxi-way. In the background center may be seen the underground revetments that were used for the protection of some of Atsugi's "Jacks."

Dominating the picture are the shining fighter planes. We see a "piece," at least, of virtually all of the 7th Fighter Squadron's P-38s as they existed at the end of the Pacific War. There was no longer the need of aircraft dispersal, there was no longer the hustle and bustle that had been seen among a squadron of fighter planes—fuel trucks, armorers, mechanics, radio and IFF men, crew chiefs and pilots. It was all over, and I feel that this particular scene epitomizes just that.

Looking back to the "Last Roundup" photographs for a moment, I remember standing there and watching the work of the bulldozers. Squadrons of planes were in the process of being demolished, and I thought to myself, thank God it is not the other way around, and you know what I mean. At the risk of editorializing I must firmly and simply say just this: our Country, the United States of America, must always remain strong if it always is to remain free.

During my Pacific "tour" I took quite a few photos—enough to help make up, upon my return home, four scrap books. One of these four was devoted only to aircraft of Japan. To aid my cause, my parents diligently combed the city of Baltimore to gather up a roll or two of film, which they promptly mailed to me. I thanked them by mail as I received the film, and I thank them again now for sending those rolls to me. There would be no scrapbooks, nor this book without them and their help.

POSTSCRIPT (1972)

When I was working on the segment of the book about the Nakajima Ki-87 "Big Boy," my curiosity became aroused: Was that handsome-looking plane still in existence? I could think of but one place to turn and that was to the venerable Smithsonian Institution in Washington, D. C. A reply to my inquiry by return mail informed me that the Ki-87 had been brought to the United States. However, the note went on to say that, in the late 1940's, it had been scrapped.

The author of this reply was the Japanese aviation historian, Robert Mikesh. I would be remiss if I did not tell you that not only is Mr. Mikesh talented and very capable in his chosen interest, but, added to this, he possesses the fine quality of being most gracious. This characteristic tempted me to press my need for help one step further. My need was the answer to the classic question: "Where are they now?" Yielding to temptation, I asked, "What Japanese warbirds are in the United States now (the summer of '72) and where are these planes?"

Breaking down the carefully prepared charts I received into paragraph form, I submit a picture that looks like this. At Willow Grove Naval Air Station, near Philadelphia, there are three Japanese planes. I have had the pleasure of seeing and also photographing them as they stand on exhibit. They are a B6N1 "Jill," a N1K1 "Rex," and a N1K2 "George." There are two other "Rexes" in the U.S. One is at Norfolk NAS and belongs to the National Air and Space Museum. The other belongs to the U. S. Navy for the Battleship USS Alabama. There are two additional "Georges," one at the NAS at Norfolk and the other belongs to the Air Force Museum at Dayton, Ohio.

The Planes of Fame Museum at Buena Park, California possesses several Japanese aircraft. There are two A6M5 "Zekes" on hand. Also there are a J2M3 "Jack," a J8M1 (rocket fighter), and, last but not at least, there is the only flyable Japanese fighter plane in the States, a Ki-84 "Frank." The National Air and Space Museum has in storage (some of which are boxed) at Silver Hill, Maryland several Japanese warplanes. There are a Ki-45 "Nick," a Ki-115 Tsurugi (Sabre), an A6M5 "Zeke," a B7A "Grace," a C6N1 "Myrt," a J1N1-S "Irving," a J7W1 Shinden (Magnificent Lightning), a M6A1 Seiran (Mountain Haze), a P1Y "Frances," a Kikka (Orange Blossom, Japan's twin-jet fighter of that period), and the nose and tail of a G4M3 "Betty." The NASM also has out on loan an A6M5 "Zeke" to the U. S. Marine Corps at Quantico, Virginia, as well as a Ki-43 "Oscar" to the Experimental Aircraft Association at Franklin, Wisconsin for exhibit.

NEW MATERIAL

Meatballs and Dead Birds became an instant classic when it was first published in the early 1970s because of its incredible collection of rare and amazing photographs of Japanese aircraft. When the opportunity to republish the book came up, I jumped at it, then wondered what could be done to make the book even more special. The answer was buried in James Gallagher's collection of photos—add more! Thanks are due to Barry Casanova who made this possible.

Enjoy.

Chris Evans
History Editor
August, 2004

The remains of a Japanese Army bomber, code-named "Peggy," on an airstrip near Luzon, April 1945.

A stunning collection of photographs of Japanese airfields being attacked by low-flying American bombers using parachute-retarded bombs. The photos were taken from the rear of an aircraft looking back at the destruction it had just created. The use of the parachutes was required to allow the attacking planes time to put some distance between themselves and their targets before the bombs detonated due to the extremely low altitude the bomb runs were made at.

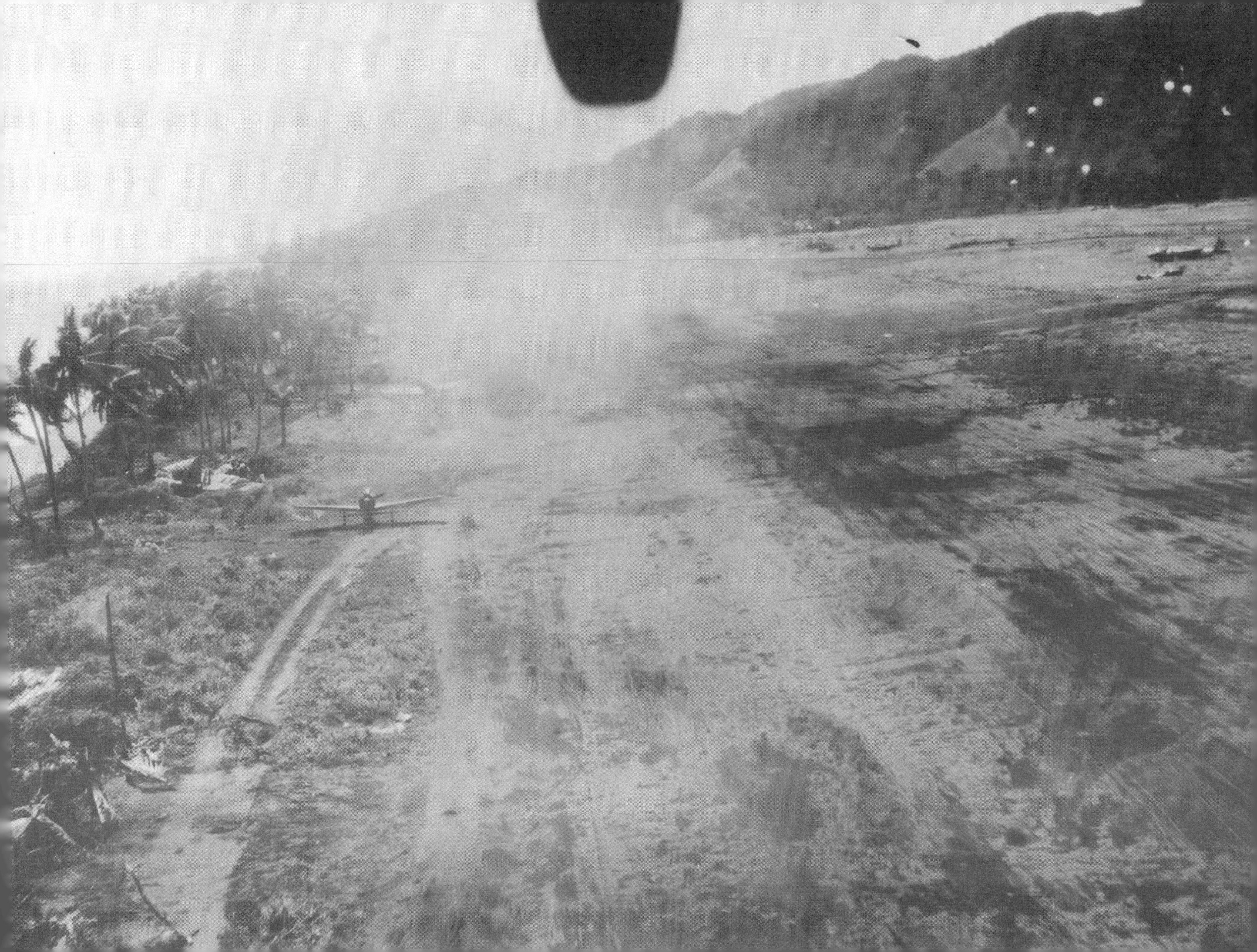

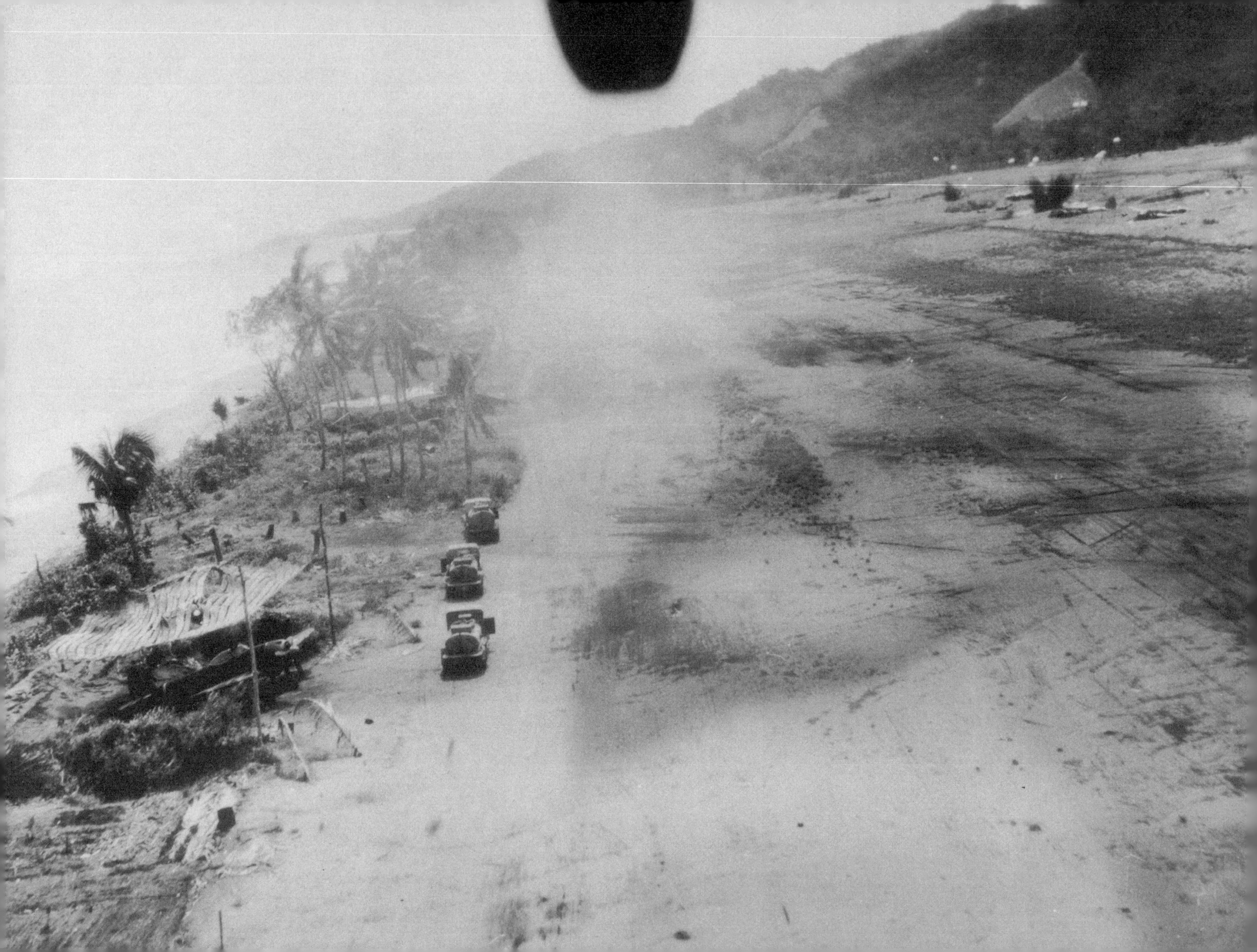

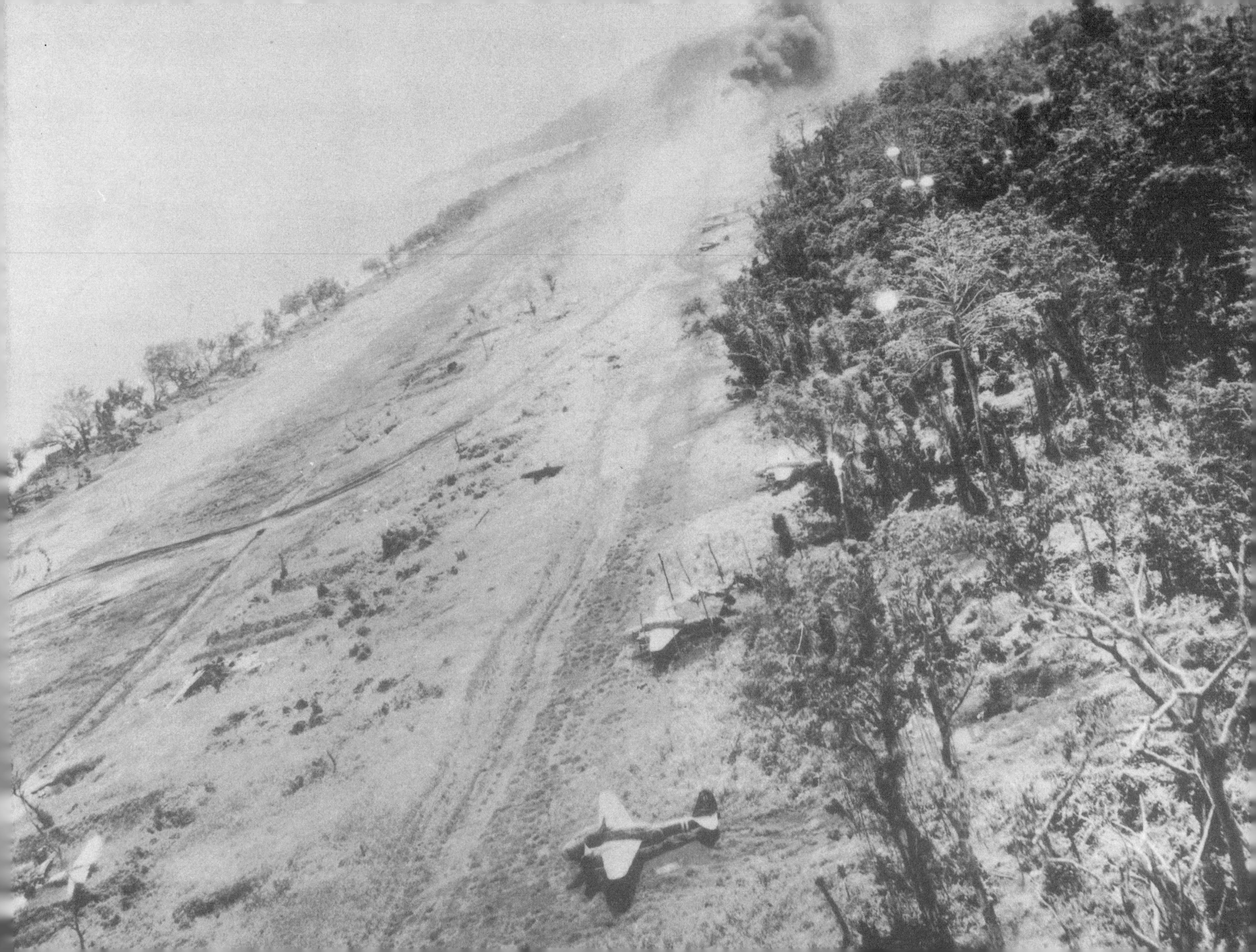

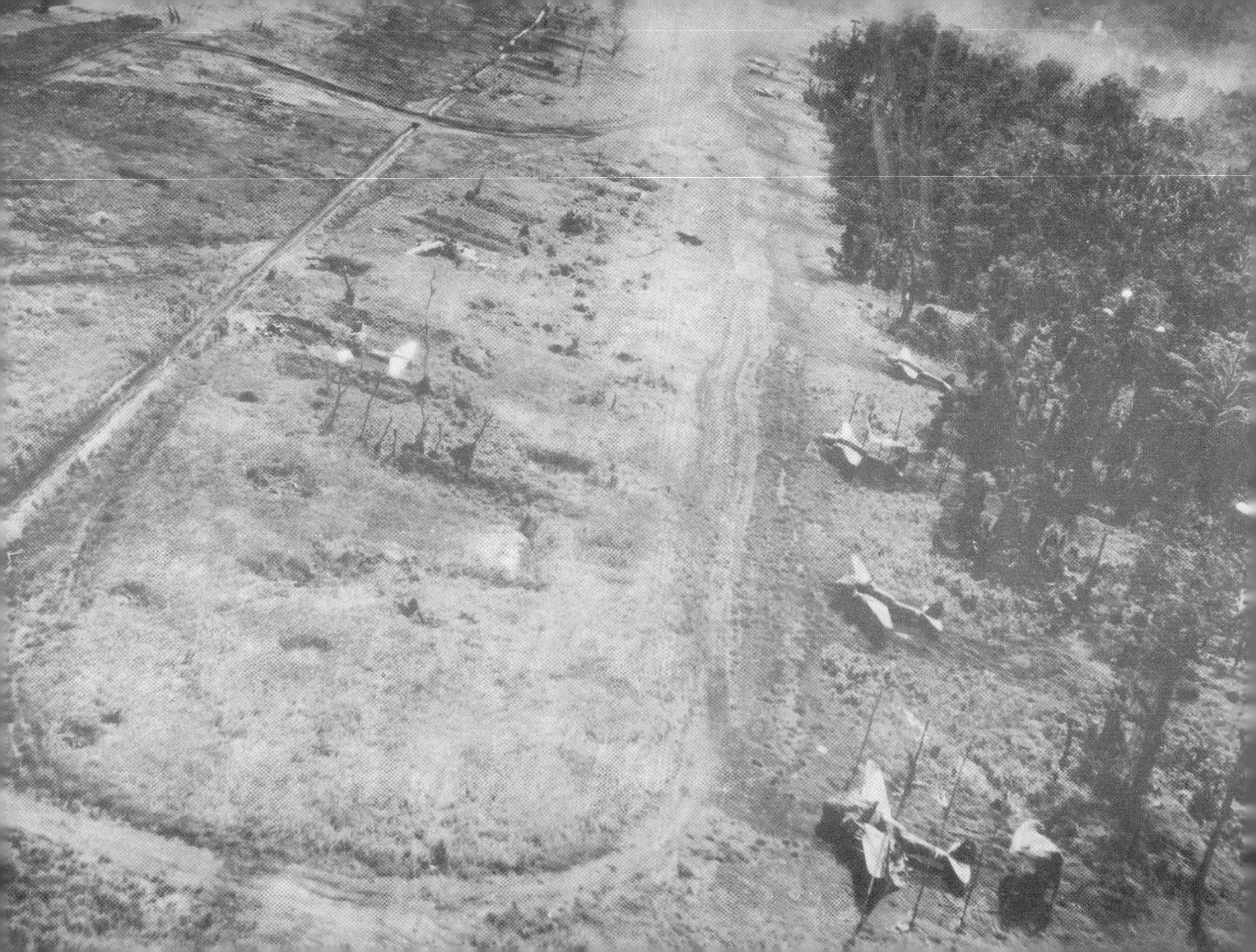

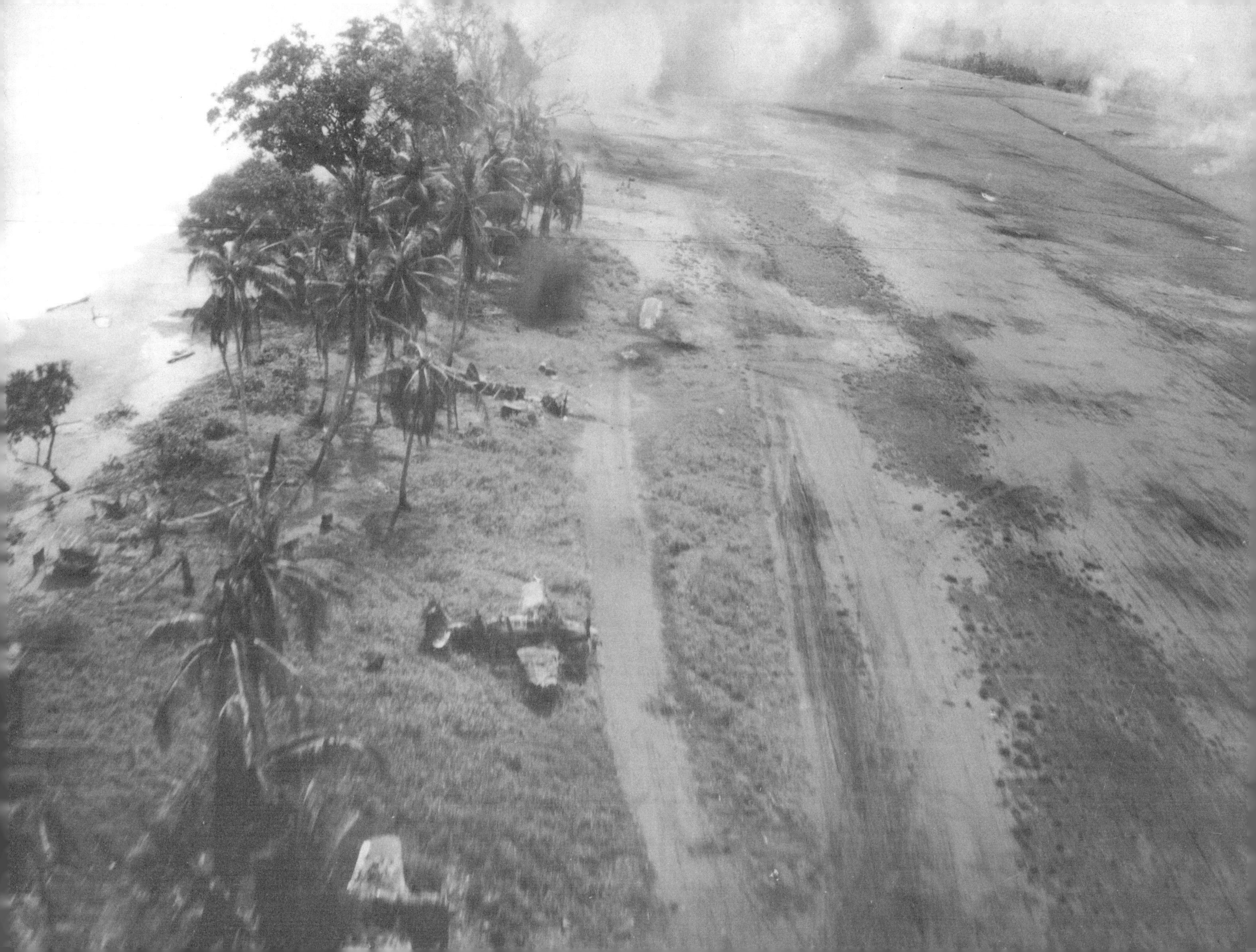

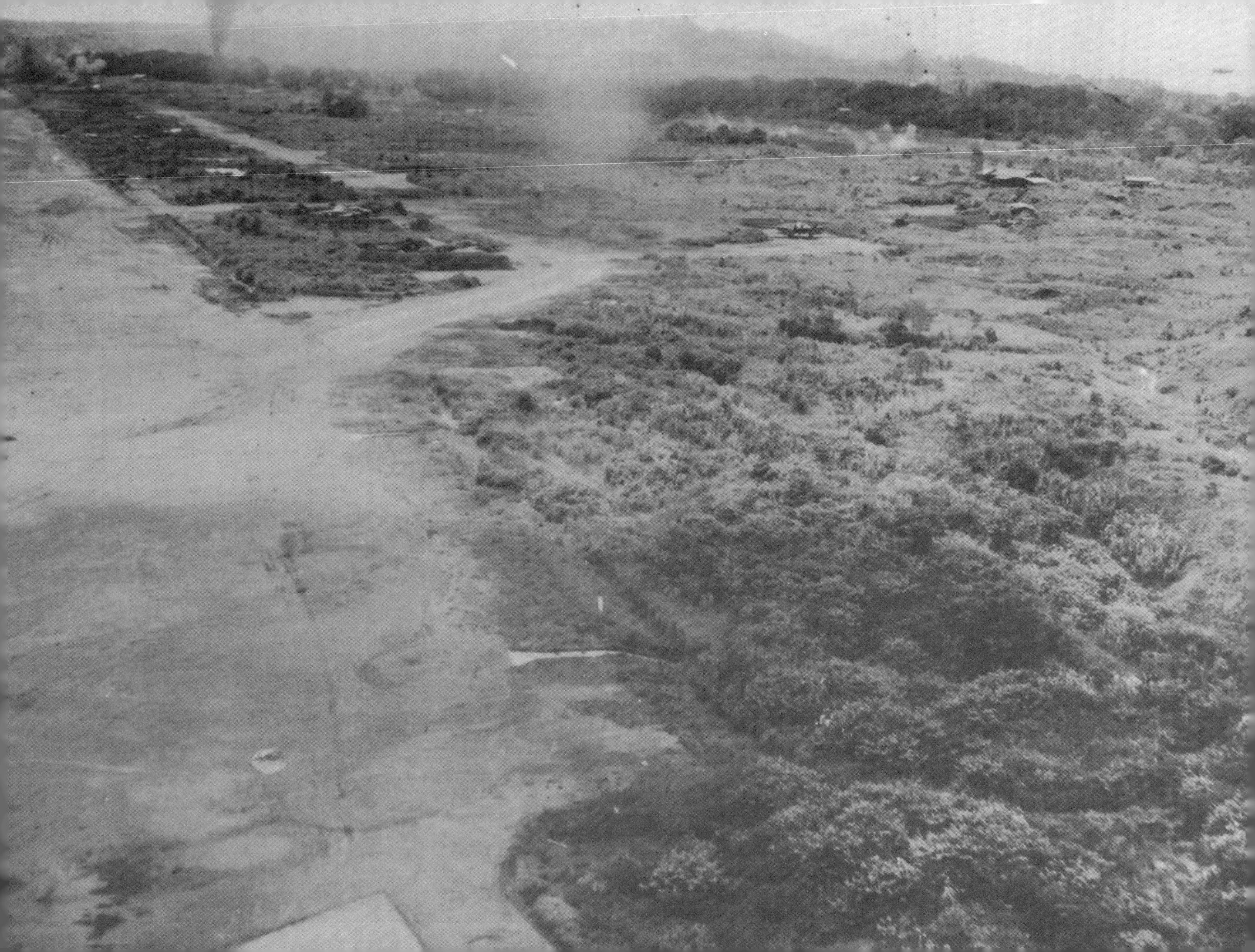

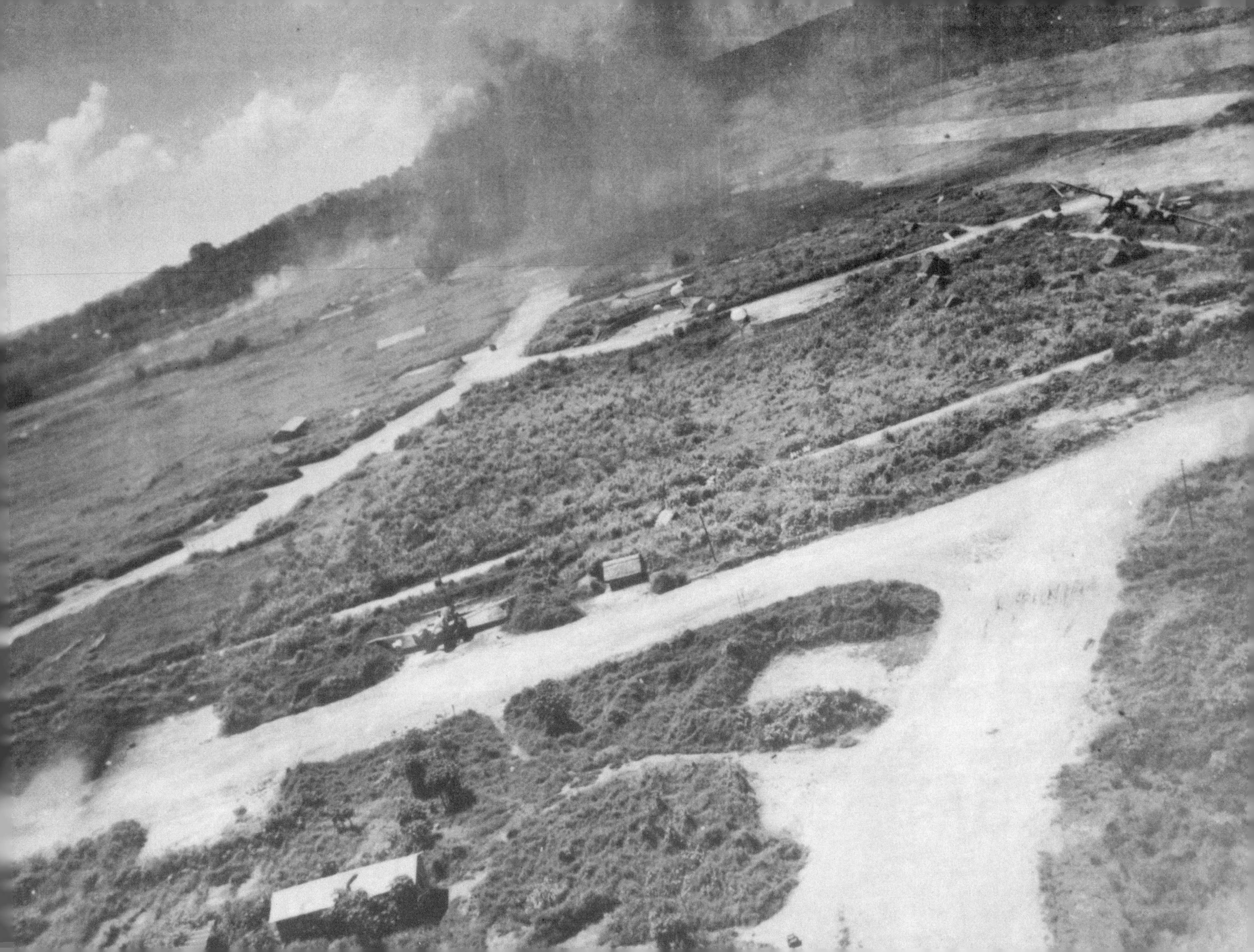

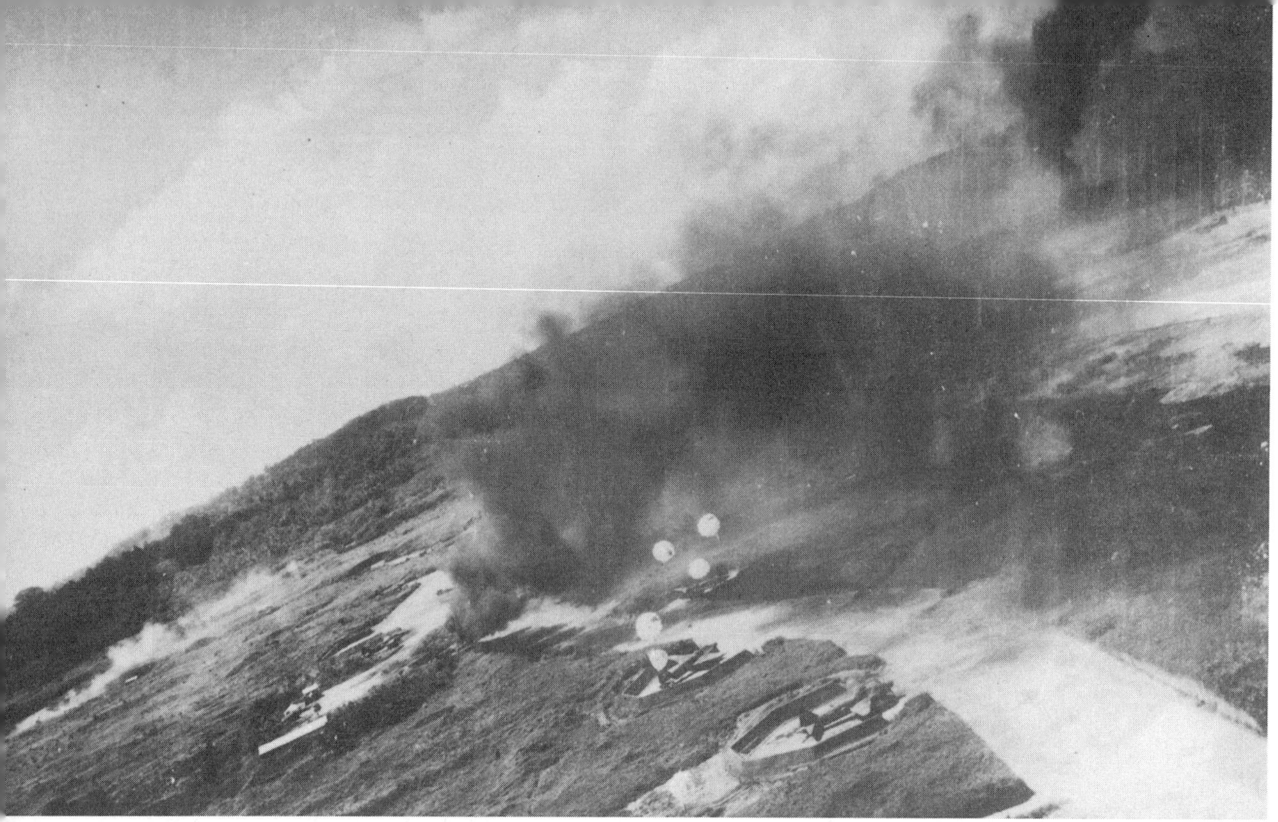

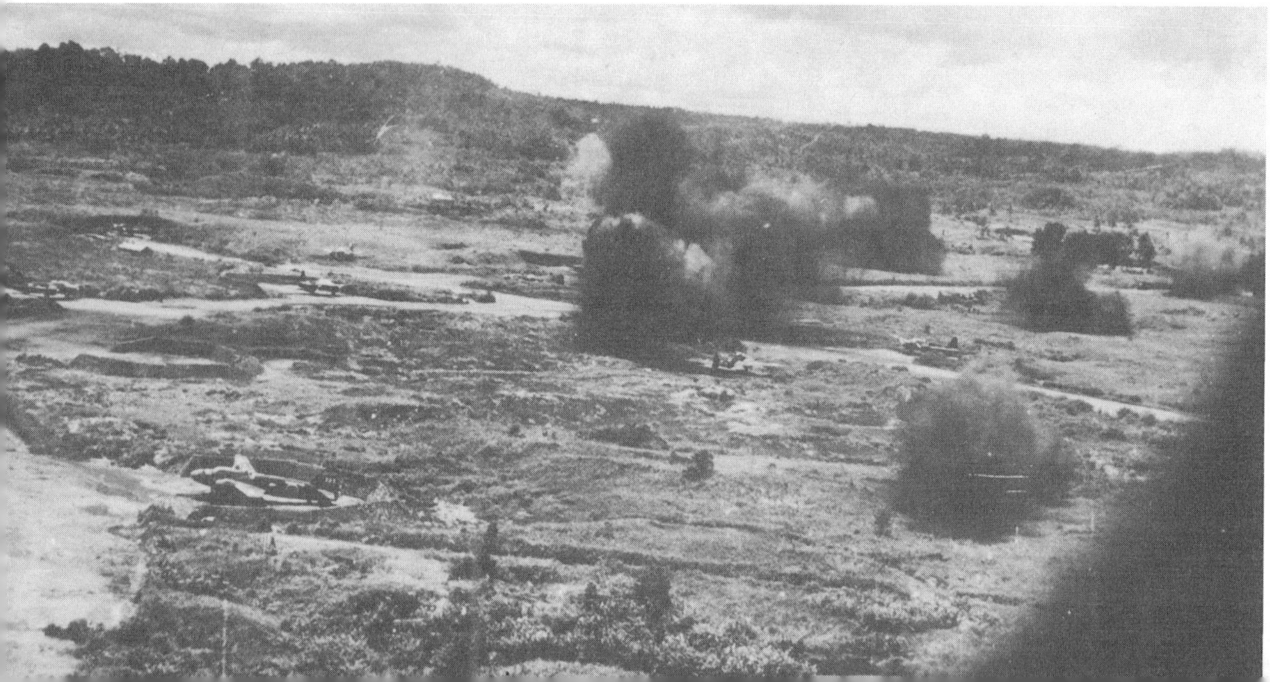

Captured Japanese anti-aircraft guns. In the second photo, Cpl. "Pop" Dawson from Florida checks out one of the guns captured by the Marines on Cape Gloucester, New Britain, February 1944.

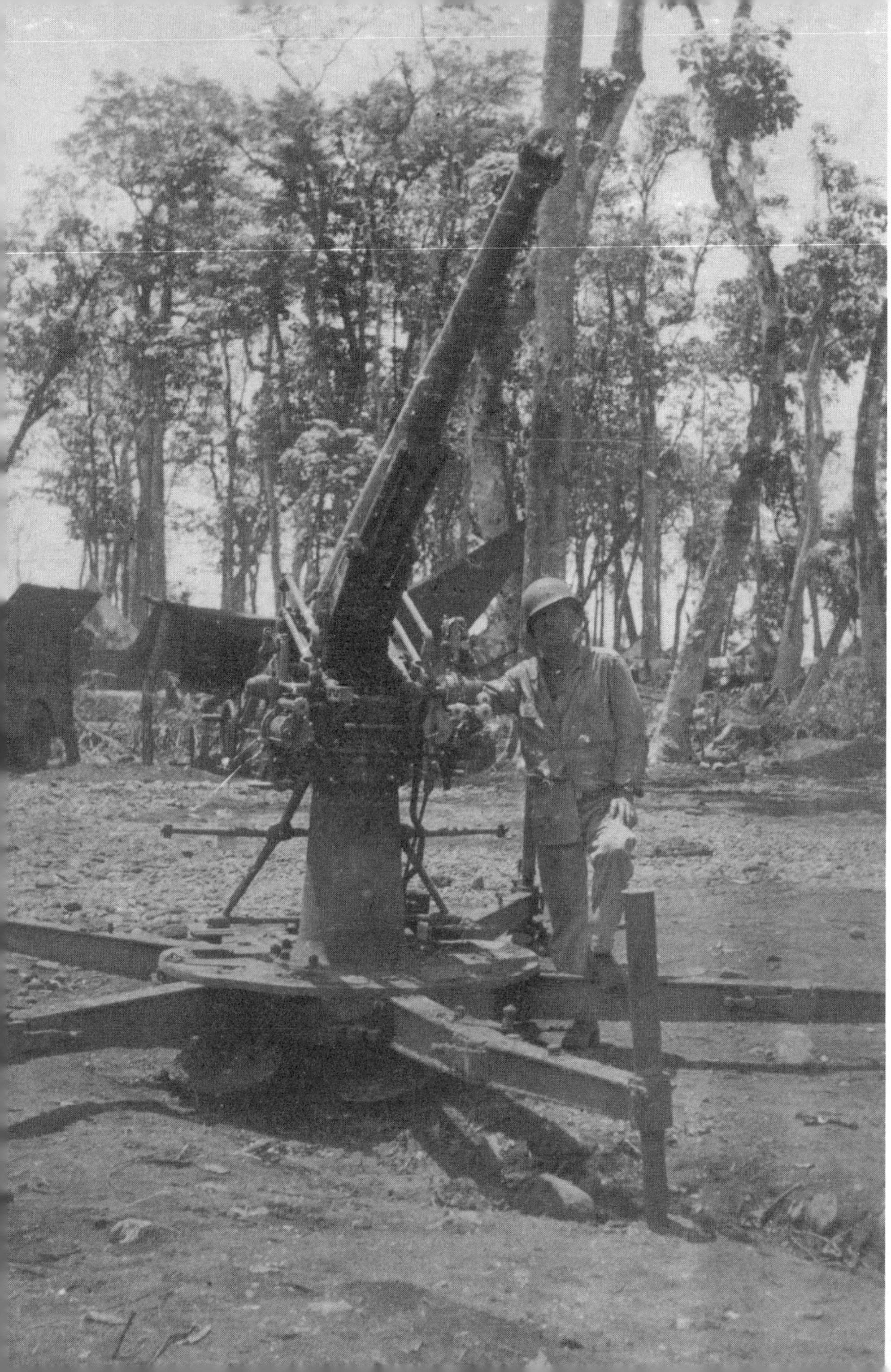

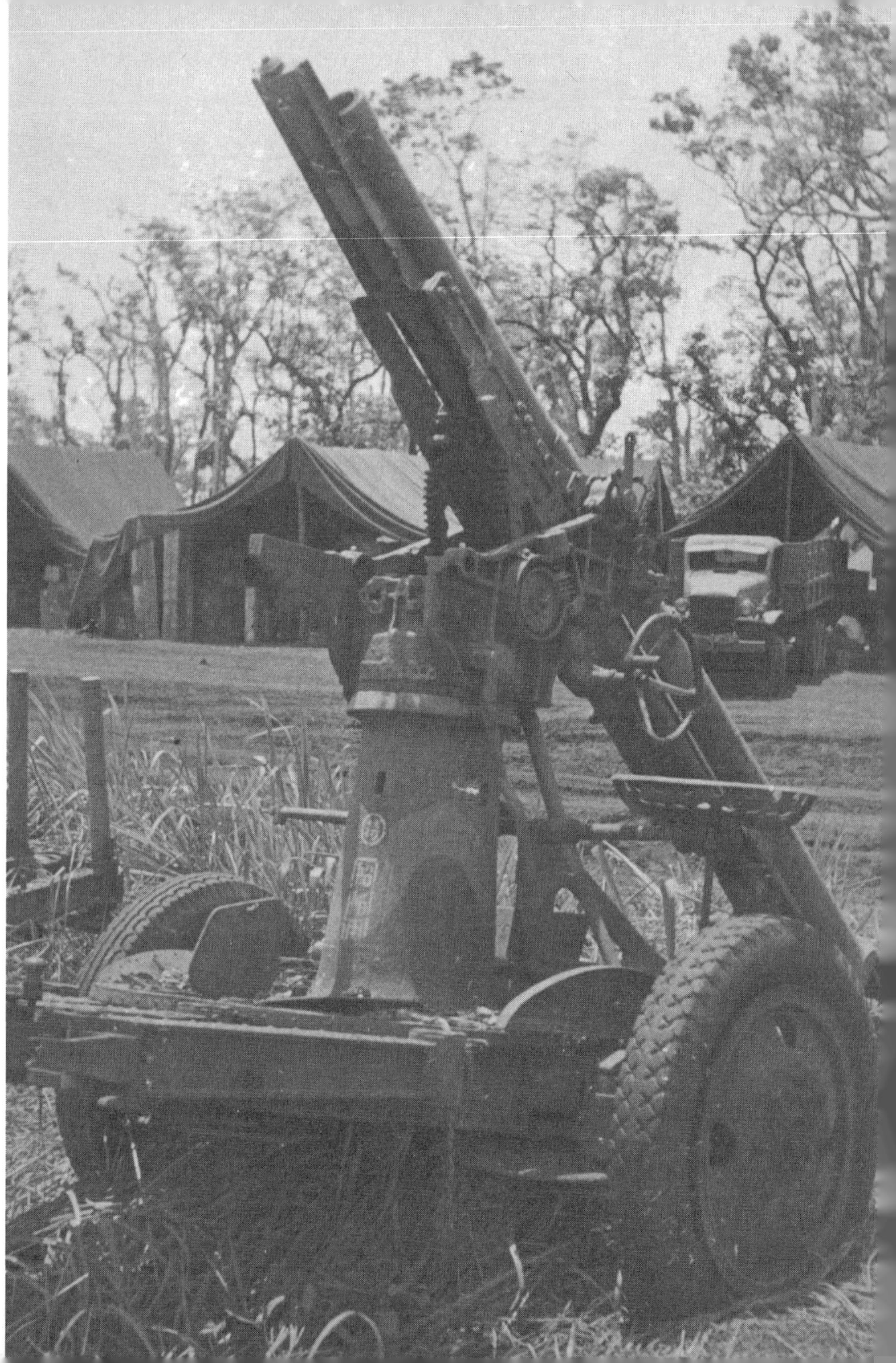

For a bit of balance, here are three shots of USAAF P-61 Black Widows put out to pasture at Atsugi, Honshu, Japan, October 1945.

154 *New Material*

The sad remains of a once mighty warrior. The final days of a Zero as it passes into history, unnoticed by the P-38 squadron that now occupies its former airstrip.

ABOUT THE AUTHOR

How many of us dream—and talk—year after year about writing a book on our experiences or special interests and never have the time, energy or ability to fulfill those dreams. James P. Gallagher is one of those rare and dedicated men who managed to realize his goal. He has not only written the book he has wanted to do, he has also taken the pictures for it and arranged for the book's publication as well.

During World War II he became fascinated with Japanese aircraft and began photographing as much as he could before the remaining planes were destroyed by the Occupation Forces. A prize-winning amateur photographer since his college days, he began taking pictures during the war with the vague intention of making a scrapbook. He lost his camera when an Australian bomber, on which he was hitching a ride, crashed off the coast of New Guinea near Aitape. This qualified him for membership in the Goldfish Club, which is restricted to those who survived a crash landing at sea by using a life raft. The lost camera was replaced by an obsolete folding f 6.3 Kodak with a speed up to only 1/50th of a second—a camera dug out of the family attic by his brother.

With this dilapidated camera Jim Gallagher lovingly photographed as many types of Japanese aircraft as he could locate in the Tokyo-Yokohama area. The best and most unusual pictures from his collection are reproduced in *Meatballs and Dead Birds*. None of these has been published before. All but four were made in Japan. The others were made in the Philippines.

They were taken when the author-photographer was a member of the United States Army Air Forces. A native Baltimorean, he enlisted after graduating from Loyola College in 1942. As a Communications Officer he served twenty-five months in the Pacific under General Douglas MacArthur's command. He participated in six campaigns: the Bismarck Archipelago, New Guinea, Leyte, Luzon, Western Pacific, and the Air Offensive Against Japan. The 49th Fighter Group was the first Air Force unit to return to the Philippines, and as a member of that group, he shared in the Presidential Unit Citation awarded for its work in the Leyte Campaign. The 49th was the first Air Force unit to be based in Japan.

Jim Gallagher worked on this book for more than two years, and it became his labor of love.

Harold A. Williams
Editor
Baltimore Sunday Sun